MW01036169

DISTRACTED

BY LISA LOOMER

★

★

DRAMATISTS
PLAY SERVICE
INC.

DISTRACTED
Copyright © 2009, Lisa Loomer

All Rights Reserved

SPECIAL NOTE

SPECIAL NOTE ON SONGS AND RECORDINGS

ACKNOWLEDGMENTS

Thank you to Elizabeth Stone for the line, "When you have a child, it's like having your heart walking around outside your body." Thanks to Dr. Lawrence Diller, Dr. Jim Blechman, and Jesse Philips for their insight and wisdom. Thanks to Leonard Foglia, Liz Diamond, Mark Brokaw and all the actors who helped shape the play. Thanks to Joe Romano (*mil grazie*), and to Marcello Romano for the music.

PRODUCTION NOTES

ON CASTING

The multiple casting is specific and should not change. Three of the actors (who do not play family and neighbors) play the experts and helpers. The multiple casting often makes an actor play characters with opposing points of view.

The casting can be multi-racial, but the picture must make sense in terms of who represents the Powers That Be. The neighborhood is middle to upper middle class, and the audience should feel this is happening in their city or town.

ON PRODUCTION

The set is minimal in terms of furniture, but wired to evoke our ADD world. A world of screens. Set pieces should be flexible and move easily. A kitchen counter can also be Mama's desk. Chairs can shoot on and off. A bed might be more suggested than literal. That said, a certain amount of "business" is a good idea so we have a sense of the fabric of real life, and Mama and Dad will need props in the kitchen. Mama should be making breakfast or a sandwich, say, as she talks to the audience.

How much the screens, themselves, draw attention is a delicate balance. They should be behind or to the side of the action so as not to interfere with a scene. When the play was done in the round, TV screens were hung above the action.

Different locales are evoked by these ever-changing screens. Outside, the screens might be blue sky or some detail symbolizing the neighborhood. The Impressionist posters in the various shrinks' offices are also projected on screens, and these should be the more familiar Impressionist images in order to support the text. Van Gogh's self-portrait should be one of the lighter ones.

There are times when the screens need to be specific to the text, as when Bush appears on TV, for example, in three close-ups. I have

4

been specific about where and how video and sound work, having seen a number of productions. I have also been specific about how long a shot on TV or film lasts, as too much video can easily overwhelm a production.

The TV remains on (moving) only in Scene 15, and, possibly Scene 8 where a game plays in the background. But the sound should be lowered quickly so as not to interfere with the scene. The slower the action on TV, the better. Since the TV screen is upstage of the character watching, he or she can look "out" at the image that we are seeing behind him. When Mama and Dad are in their cars in Scene 5, moving video of traffic works fine.

For the most part, there is little or no pause between scenes, and transitions are seamless. Often, Jesse calls out the new scene as if it were the last line in the previous scene. Furniture pieces move in and out under dialogue. A grilled-cheese sandwich does not have to be made in "real time." This is an ADD world, and ADD moves fast.

Music should be the kind that Jesse listens to: frenetic, with a strong beat; hip hop or rap.

OTHER THOUGHTS ON THE PLAY

The audience, for Mama, is someone who actually has the time to listen. In Scene 1, she's just met the audience, so she tries to keep the best possible face on things with Jesse, as you would with a new friend. Mama's got a big story to tell, so it's important for the journey of the play that Mama remains positive throughout, always searching, looking for "answers" that will help her son. Of course, there are places where she reacts to hard news, but these must be chosen carefully for the energy of the story to sustain. Even when she's shocked, thrown, or disappointed, she still seeks to justify, to question, or to find the next step … all positive objectives. The same is largely true for Dad. Only after the second scene in New Mexico, do they pause, completely at a loss as to what to do next. And what Mama comes to in the final scene, is not a "solution" … just a first step on the next part of their journey.

Most productions have Jesse on tape till the final scene. It is important that he announce each new scene either with great energy or with a particular attitude about the scene. We need the sense from his first "SCENE ONE!" that all his emotions are a bit larger than life.

I have seen a number of productions and would be happy to share more thoughts with a director by email: peter.hagan@abramsartny.com.

DISTRACTED was originally produced by Center Theater Group at the Mark Taper Forum (Michael Ritchie, Artistic Director; Charles Dillingham, Managing Director), in Los Angeles, California, opening on March 25, 2007. It was directed by Leonard Foglia; the set design and projections were by Elaine J. McCarthy; the costume design was by Robert Blackman; the lighting design was by Russell H. Champa; the sound design was by Jon Gottlieb; and the production stage manager was David S. Franklin. The cast was as follows:

MAMA	Rita Wilson
DAD	Ray Porter
JESSE	Hudson Thames
DR. ZAVALA, DR. BRODER, DR. JINKS, DR. KARNES	Bronson Pinchot
MRS. HOLLY, DR. WALLER, CAROLYN, NURSE, WAITRESS	Stephanie Berry
SHERRY	Marita Geraghty
VERA	Johanna Day
NATALIE	Emma Hunton

DISTRACTED was subsequently produced Off-Broadway by the Roundabout Theatre Company (Todd Haimes, Artistic Director) at the Laura Pels Theatre, opening on February 7, 2009. It was directed by Mark Brokaw; the set design was by Mark Wendland; the costume design was by Michael Krass; the lighting design was by Jane Cox; the original music and sound design were by David Van Tieghem; the projections and video were by Tal Yarden; and the production stage manager was William H. Lang. The cast was as follows:

MAMA	Cynthia Nixon
DAD	Josh Stamberg
JESSE	Matthew Gumley
DR. ZAVALA, WAITRESS, CAROLYN	Natalie Gold
MRS. HOLLY, DR. WALLER, NURSE	Aleta Mitchell
DR. BRODER, DR. JINKS, DR. KARNES	Peter Benson
SHERRY	Mimi Lieber
VERA	Lisa Emery
NATALIE	Shana Dowdeswell

CHARACTERS
Nine actors play the following roles:

MAMA — Smart, warm, wry, 30s or early 40s. An unfailingly positive person who keeps her her ironic sense of humor (as long as possible!) and will go to any lengths to help her son.

DAD — A guy's guy, 30s or 40s, bright, with quick impulses. Working class background, designs car crashes. Easygoing — till pushed — and even then the tone of his anger is more incredulous than dark.

JESSE — Funny, wild, sweet, impulsive, impatient, exuberant, angry, with a mouth on him, 9. Mostly an offstage voice, but a big one.

DR. ZAVALA — A child psychologist, 30s. Very sensitive, dedicated and eager to help, but a bit anxious herself. She might be rather new at her job.

MRS. HOLLY — An overworked school teacher for twenty-two years. Strong and straight-ahead. African American. 40s or 50s.

DR. WALLER — An educational neuropsychologist going through a hard time. Played by the actress who plays Mrs. Holly.

DR. DANIEL BRODER — A wise, warm, and compassionate homeopath. Laid-back, just trying to lead a healthy life in a toxic world. Might have a New York accent.

SHERRY — A well-off suburban mother who wants the very best for her kids. Covers her pain with a smile and chases it with a doughnut.

VERA — A neighbor with no people skills, obsessive-compulsive, pointed, and direct. But she does try to be helpful! When Vera's gathering information, we have no idea how she feels about the questions she asks — or about the answers she receives. Way down deep? She's looking for a little validation.

NATALIE — A teenager with big mood swings. Open-hearted and angry. A cutter.

DR. JINKS — A highly respected psychiatrist. Played by the actor who plays Dr. Broder. Tightly buttoned. Might be a Brit.

CAROLYN — Mother of an autistic child. Played by the actress who plays Dr. Zavala.

DR. KARNES — An environmental physician, passionate about this new science. Played by the actor who plays Jinks and Broder. Eastern European.

ACTOR WITH ADD — Plays Dr. Broder, Dr. Jinks, and Dr. Karnes. Impulsive, explosive, and passionate about his medication. Might or might not use accents with Jinks and Broder.

NURSE — Down-to-earth, kind, from a small town in the South. Played by the actress who plays Dr. Waller and Mrs. Holly.

WAITRESS — Spacey. ADD. Played by the actress who plays Dr. Zavala.

All of these characters believe wholeheartedly in their points of view. The humor comes from a character's passion, not from caricature.

DISTRACTED

Scene 1

As the audience settles, we hear sounds of modern life — rap music, a cell phone ringing, several channels playing the news … And then sudden quiet. The stage is dark. Mama runs in, lights a candle, sits cross-legged on the floor … and meditates.

MAMA. *(Eyes closed.)* "Lord make me an instrument of thy peace. Where there is hatred, let me sow love. Where there is injury, pardon. Where there is doubt, faith … Where there is despair, hope … Where there is darkness, light … Where there is sadness, joy. O Divine Master, grant that I may not seek so much to be consoled as to console, to be understood as to understand, to be loved as to love. For it is in giving that we receive, it is in pardoning that we are pardoned, it is in dying to self that we are born to eternal life." *(A voice is heard, a small voice — but loud.)*
JESSE'S VOICE. *("Let's go!")* SCENE ONE! *(Mama opens her eyes.)*
MAMA. It's seven A.M. Soon he will be awake. I have to meditate. Fast. The way I meditate is to say the St. Francis Prayer, over and over. I love this prayer. *(Closes eyes.)* "Lord, make me an instrument of thy —" *(The phone rings. Begins again:)* "Lord, make me an instrument of thy peace." *(The phone rings.)* I'll just let the voicemail get it — *(Meditates.)* "Where there is hatred, let me sow love, where there is injury — *(Phone rings. Bit annoyed:)* pardon." *(Opens eyes.)* You know, I've been getting these calls lately that say, "Please hold for an important — *(The phone rings. She doesn't pause for it.)* message"? So naturally, I hang up immediately … But then last week, curiosity got the best of me, and it turned out to be American Express — and my bill was overdue. The man was extremely nice, said it was an "honor" to assist me, and then he asked me to stay on the line to do

11

a service rating, and since he was doing such a great job — all the way from India — I stayed on for another five minutes … and had no time to meditate. So. *(Meditates.)* "Where there is doubt, faith — " *(Notices.)* My knees hurt. *(Meditates.)* "Where there is despair, hope — " *(Phone rings.)* You know, what if it isn't American Express? What if it's important? *(She rises and gets the phone.)* Hello? … No, I don't want a lower rate on cable TV. I like paying the higher rate, thank you so much. *(She hangs up and sits down to meditate.)* "Lord, make me an instrument of thy — " *(Again — the voice!)*

JESSE. MOM!

MAMA. *(Determined.)* "Lord — "

JESSE. MAMA!

MAMA. "Lord — "

JESSE. *(Pissed off.)* MOOOOOM!

MAMA. *(Whispers; sneaking it in.)* "Lord — " *(Rises; gives up.)* Fuck it. *(Lights come up. Set pieces fly on, an assault of kitchen stuff. Toys might be flung onstage. This house is a mess. Mama starts to get breakfast ready. Calls offstage; optimistic:)* Morning, Jess! Are you dressed? *(No answer.)* Are you getting dressed, baby?

JESSE. I'm dressed!

MAMA. Get dressed, Jesse —

JESSE. Whatever, dude.

MAMA. *(To audience.)* He's nine. By the way — I'm keeping him offstage, because, well … I don't think the stage is a particularly healthy place for a child. Besides, people only want to see a child onstage if he's singing show tunes.

JESSE. Where the hell are my rocket balloons?

MAMA. *(Embarrassed; smiles.)* Don't say hell, Jess. And they're your toys, babe, you find 'em. What do you want for breakfast?

JESSE. Candy.

MAMA. *(Laughs; to audience.)* Sure, I'd love a couple of Almond Joys myself! *(Calls.)* Well, you can't, 'cause it's not good for you.

JESSE. Whatever, dude —

MAMA. So what do you want?

JESSE. *(Shouts; exasperated.)* Poached eggs! Whatever!

MAMA. *(Lightly.)* And when they're done, he changes his mind. He gets Cocoa Crispies, and after he has filled it too high with milk, and spilled it on the floor, he finds a rocket balloon, and, instead of eating, he gets … distracted. *(Mama starts making his lunch.)*

JESSE. I gotta find the pump to the rocket balloons!

MAMA. Well, it's time to get dressed now —

JESSE. I never get dressed before I eat!

MAMA. All right, eat then.

JESSE. Lemme just find the pump!

MAMA. We're not setting off rocket balloons!

JESSE. *(Explodes.)* I don't want to set them off! I just want to find the fucking pump*! (A pause. Mama smiles at the audience, embarrassed.)*

MAMA. All right, find it. And then get dressed and eat — or eat and get dressed, whatever. *(To audience.)* I know. I should have given one simple command. I should have given a "time out" for the word "fucking." But I said "All right, find the pump" for two reasons. First of all, I've just meditated and I think of myself as an instrument of peace. Also, I've just read a book called *The Explosive Child,* which says you should pick your battles. You should have an A basket for issues of safety, a C basket for issues that are not important right now, and a B basket for the negotiables. The book says that you should model flexibility for your child, so he knows he can get what *he* wants *and* I can get what I want. Right now, I want him to get to school without a tantrum. And I want to read the news. *(She goes to her computer and reads current headlines — which also appear on screen.)* Another bombing, sixty-seven killed. Floods ravage the Northwest … *(Dad enters, checking his cell, finishing getting dressed, and starting to make a grilled cheese, as Mama continues reading.)* Dow's down three hundred points … *(Mutters.)* Locusts? Plague? Hey, remember that guy who sued his wife for a kidney in their divorce? There's an article —

DAD. I know. I read it in the bathroom.

MAMA. Apparently, he'll settle for a kidney or the cash equivalent —

DAD. You know, it's ten to eight and he's not dressed?

MAMA. What are you doing?

DAD. Making him a grilled cheese.

MAMA. Why?

DAD. Because that's what he'll eat.

MAMA. *(To audience.)* And then he does something I would never do —

DAD. *(Yells upstairs.)* Get dressed, Jess, or I'm dropping you off at school in your pajamas.

JESSE. *(Upset.)* OKAY ALREADY! *(Dad sticks the sandwich in the microwave.)*

13

MAMA. *(To audience.)* Our son does not like to get dropped off. He likes to get walked in. He's a little … anxious.

DAD. He's fine.

MAMA. *(To audience.)* At least that's what the psychologist who observed him a few weeks ago at school thought —

DAD. *(Laughs.)* Bullshit!

MAMA. Does that mean you won't be joining me for our session today?

DAD. *(Lightly.)* Baby, I gotta work! *(He takes the sandwich out of the microwave and sticks it in a paper towel.)*

MAMA. My husband designs crash tests — *(He gets his briefcase, bumping into something on the way.)*

DAD. Shit — *(Calls.)* I'm leaving, Jess! I'll be in the car!

JESSE. Hold on!

MAMA. *(To audience.)* You know, I thought of doing this as a one woman thing … But I couldn't get them out of my head. I couldn't get them quiet enough. *(Smiles at Dad.)* I mean, I could get *him* out of my head sometimes — *(He kisses her goodbye.)*

DAD. Love you.

MAMA. *(Loving; if rushed.)* Love you, bye.

DAD. *(Yells to Jesse.)* I'm in the car! *(He exits.)*

MAMA. But your kid … Even when he goes to school … I heard someone say that when you have a child, it's like having your heart walking around outside your body.

JESSE. *(Anxious.)* What if there's a fire drill?

MAMA. *(Reassuring.)* Get under the desk, you'll be fine. *(Remembers.)* Wait! That's the bomb drill. Don't get under the desk, get in line with the other kids and go outside.

JESSE. I don't like the noise! *(Loud staccato siren noise.)* ENH-ENH-ENH-ENH —

MAMA. Just do what the teacher tells you!

JESSE. *(Imitating teacher.)* Attention, students. Stop, drop, roll. ENH-ENH-ENH-ENH —

MAMA. *(Encouraging.)* See? You know what to do.

JESSE. Bye, Mom!

MAMA. Have a good day! *(Looks at watch; to audience.)* I have seven hours till he gets home. It's time to get to my *new* job —

JESSE. Hold on. Just let me get a CD!

MAMA. Finding his diagnosis — *(To him.)* No rap, Jesse! *(To audience.)* I meant to say this in the beginning —

JESSE. Where the hell's my iPod?
MAMA. But I got … distracted.
JESSE. Bye, Mom! Don't forget me!
MAMA. I won't!
JESSE. ENH, ENH, ENH, ENH — SCENE TWO!

Scene 2

Kitchen pieces start to disappear, a desk comes on, or the counter turns into a desk.

MAMA. Since I've just quit my job as an interior designer to work at home and focus on my child, I wonder if I should just sneak in a little work for my one freelance client — *(She gets the phone and a notebook marked "Jesse.")* But decide to call that doctor about Jesse instead. *(Sits.)* Dr. Waller is the neuropsychologist recommended by the psychologist our pediatrician recommended, when Jesse decided to crash toy cars instead of having his ears, throat, and testicles examined during a recent physical. *(Calling.)* And since she'll be the one to make a diagnosis … I'm kind of hoping to get her machine. *(Dr. Waller enters, on her phone, with her office chair. She is very upset. We see a projection establishing her office, an Impressionist print.)*
DR. WALLER. *(Fighting tears.)* I'm sorry, who is this?
MAMA. Jesse Cara's mother? *(To audience.)* I add the little question mark so as not to seem too aggressive. *(To Waller.)* I've left a couple of messages…?
DR. WALLER. Oh yes. Can you hold a sec? *(She goes back to her other call, furious. Yells into phone:)* Take the damn Lexus, but you will *not* get my dog! *(Switches to Mama; professional.)* I'm sorry I haven't gotten back to you. I had a bit of an emergency.
MAMA. *(To audience.)* How do you have a "bit" of an emergency? *(To Dr. Waller.)* I'm so sorry. I hope everything is all right?
DR. WALLER. *(Bit too emphatic.)* Fine!
MAMA. *(To audience.)* I wonder about her emergency …
DR. WALLER. *(To herself.)* I wish she'd just get on with it so I could go cry!

15

MAMA. Our psychologist, Dr. Zavala, recommended you for neuropsych testing?

DR. WALLER. Dr. Zavala? I've never heard of Dr. Zavala. Can you tell me a little about your concerns?

MAMA. Do you have time right now?

DR. WALLER. *(Fighting tears.)* Yes …

MAMA. So I tell her about my talk last week with Dr. Zavala. *(Dr. Zavala enters, in her office chair, and sits on the other side of Mama, so Mama is between the two doctors. Dr. Zavala's Impressionist print is projected. Dr. Zavala has a laptop or Blackberry with notes, and consults it often, not wanting to make a mistake. We see the session with Dr. Zavala that took place a week ago, which Mama is describing to Dr. Waller in the present.)*

DR. ZAVALA. Well, let's see … I spent about three hours observing him at school … I watched him in class, in P.E. … at lunch … I also spoke with his teacher —

MAMA. *(To audience.)* At a hundred twenty-five an hour plus travel time —

DR. ZAVALA. And from what I observed … He is a pretty anxious child.

DR. WALLER. *(On phone; to Mama.)* I see …

MAMA. *(To Dr. Zavala; anxious.)* You really think he's … anxious?

DR. ZAVALA. Yes. And he seems to try to compensate for the anxiety by being funny —

MAMA. *(Pleased.)* Really? He was funny?

DR. ZAVALA. Well — sometimes. He uses physical humor quite a lot, falling off a chair, falling off his desk, running into a wall in an effort to engage the other children —

MAMA. *(Hopeful.)* Did they laugh? *(Dr. Waller rolls her eyes.)*

DR. ZAVALA. Well — sometimes. But he really can't rely on this as a way to connect to other kids. And often, he'd just go off on his own.

DR. WALLER. I see.

DR. ZAVALA. *(Looks at notes; sadly.)* He ate his lunch alone.

MAMA. He did? Oh God.

DR. ZAVALA. I'm sorry. And, like his teacher told you at your conference, he does seem to be easily … distracted.

MAMA. *(To audience.)* Our parent-teacher conference was seven weeks ago. Which is what clued us in there was a problem, which is why we — *(Dad enters with two small classroom chairs and joins Mama for the conference.)*

DAD. Not we.

MAMA. I — called Dr. Zavala. *(She turns to the actress playing Dr. Waller.)*

MAMA. Could you just be the teacher now? So we could just quickly —

ACTRESS PLAYING DR. WALLER. Now!?

MAMA. Like — like Windows. Could we just minimize Dr. Waller a sec?

ACTRESS PLAYING DR. WALLER. I guess … *(Dr. Waller rises, becoming Mrs. Holly with a slight costume adjustment. Waller's Impressionist print minimizes and a blackboard with a class schedule takes its place. Dr. Zavala relates only to Mama, in their session. Dad relates to Mama and Mrs. Holly in the parent-teacher conference. Mama goes back and forth.)*

MRS. HOLLY. Well, one of the problems is that he doesn't want to do the work. He says he hates reading, he hates writing, and he hates math.

DR. ZAVALA. *(To Mama.)* But I don't think that's really the case. I think he may just be anxious.

MRS. HOLLY. We're trying to find out what he's interested in. But right now he's not interested in anything.

DAD. He's interested in cars —

DR. ZAVALA. *(To Mama.)* He may just be too anxious to focus.

MRS. HOLLY. There was also an incident in the bathroom.

DR. ZAVALA. *(A very bad sign.)* Oh.

MRS. HOLLY. He was opening the doors on the other kids!

DR. ZAVALA. Bathroom trauma at this age is not a good thing.

MAMA. I know.

DAD. *(To Holly.)* But last week kids were looking under the stalls at *him!*

MRS. HOLLY. Well, I didn't see that. I do have twenty-seven other children in the class to keep an eye on.

MAMA. But when there's a problem, you do often seem to notice *him* … *(To audience.)* I thought I said that very nicely —

MRS. HOLLY. Well, the problem *is* often him.

DR. ZAVALA. My guess is, that with the bathroom incident, he was compensating by doing the very thing that made *him* anxious. It seems to be his way of managing anxiety.

MRS. HOLLY. *(To Mama.)* It's probably your fault. You're a terrible mother.

MAMA. *(To audience.)* She didn't say that.

MRS. HOLLY. No, I didn't. But you're right — *(To audience.)* That's what I think.

MAMA. *(To audience.)* She *did* say —

MRS. HOLLY. You might want to get him tested for Attention Deficit Disorder.

DAD. What!

MAMA. Are you saying our child has ADD!?

MRS. HOLLY. No — *(To audience.)* I'm not allowed to say that. *(To Mama.)* I'm just saying that I've been teaching for twenty-two years and I think testing for ADD might be a good idea.

MAMA. Oh.

DAD. Well, excuse me, but I have to get back to work. *(He leaves in a huff, bumping into something.)*

MAMA. *(To Holly.)* Thank you.

MRS. HOLLY. You're very welcome. *(She starts to leave.)*

MAMA. Wait! I didn't make an appointment with Dr. Waller! *(Mrs. Holly quickly becomes Dr. Waller. The blackboard minimizes and Waller's print reappears.)*

DR. WALLER. *(In tears.)* Friday, February third! *(She runs off. Her print disappears.)*

MAMA. Great! *(Sighs; to audience.)* Nine weeks from now. I call to postpone another meeting with my one freelance client ... And head for this week's appointment with Dr. Zavala. *(Mama hangs up with Dr. Waller and turns to Dr. Zavala, whose Impressionist print appears.)*

DR. ZAVALA. So how are things going?

MAMA. Fine.

DR. ZAVALA. How's working at home? Do you miss the big office, the camaraderie ... the lunches, creative stimulation?

MAMA. *(Lies.)* Nah.

DR. ZAVALA. And how're things going with Jesse?

MAMA. Well, I guess you could say I had a little trouble with the basket system this morning in terms of the word "fucking." *(Dr. Zavala has much enthusiasm for the basket system and a keen sensitivity to the nuances of the way the word "fucking" is said — whether blurted in anger or used as an adjective or whatever.)*

DR. ZAVALA. I understand. Let's see if I can help. Now, kicking, for example, is a matter of safety and definitely goes in the A basket. With the word "fucking" ... I'd say B or C basket, depending on the family. "Fucking" doesn't literally hurt anyone, but "fucking" could get him suspended from school … And if you're churchgoers, "fucking" could be a problem for all of you. Still, if he's only blurting the word "fucking" when he's angry, it's as if the circuits in his brain are temporarily overloaded — whether due to anxiety or ADD we don't know yet — and he truly may not be able to control the impulse to say "fucking" … So I'd say we leave "fucking" for the C basket — for the moment.

MAMA. *(To audience.)* To tell you the truth, I've forgotten what the C basket is for by now, so I change the subject and tell her about our upcoming appointment with Dr. Waller.

DR. ZAVALA. Who I think is wonderful, by the way —

MAMA. Well, you recommended her —

DR. ZAVALA. *(Pleased.)* Did I? And, in the meantime, I'm going to give you the name and number of an excellent psychiatrist. *(Dr. Zavala starts looking for the information on her laptop or Blackberry.)*

MAMA. A psychiatrist!?

DR. ZAVALA. Just in case Dr. Waller's results warrant it.

MAMA. Wait a minute. Psychiatrists prescribe drugs!

DR. ZAVALA. Only when necessary. *(Dr. Zavala's having trouble with the laptop or Blackberry.)*

MAMA. Well, I'm not putting my child on drugs. In no universe am I putting my child on drugs.

DR. ZAVALA. I understand. I just want you to have the option, so you can gather as much information as possible. And they book months in advance. You can always cancel. *(Dr. Zavala gives up on technology and finds a card.)* Here we are! *(Hands card to Mama.)* Dr. David Jinks. Now, you know, some psychiatrists can appear a bit reserved … But I think he'd be an excellent match.

MAMA. Wow. Is there a Match.com for shrinks now?

DR. ZAVALA. A sense of humor is such a healthy thing. Same time next week?

MAMA. Uh — sure. *(Mama rises. Dr. Zavala leaves and her print disappears.)* On the way home, I stop at Borders and pick up a few books on ADD. *(Hundreds of books on ADD rain down on screen.)*

Night. Mama is reading in her living room.

JESSE. *(Exuberantly insistent.)* Scene Three! I'm watching *Fast and Furious!*

MAMA. No, you are not. *(Sound of clomping feet. Mama keeps trying to read.)*

JESSE. Well, I'm having a snack. Daddy said I could have s'mores! *(Dad enters.)*

MAMA. Did you say he could have s'mores before bed!?

DAD. No — I said he could have Teddy Grahams when he got into his pajamas, which he said were in the dryer?

JESSE. Liar!

DAD. Turn off the TV. I'm coming up. *(He leaves.)*

JESSE. He's such a fucking liar!

MAMA. *(Smiles at audience.)* He's tired … And so am I … So I put "fucking" in the C basket and simply say — *(To Jesse.)* You may not use the "f" word, Jesse.

JESSE. Why not?

MAMA. Because you'll get kicked out of school. *(Remembers.)* And it's not nice. Go get in your pajamas.

DAD. *(Offstage; yells to Mama.)* I am looking for them!

JESSE. *(Screaming.)* Why do I always have to get into my stupid pajamas? I'm just going to get out of them again! It's so stupid! It's such a waste of time!

MAMA. *(To audience.)* How do you explain to a nine-year-old that getting in and out of pajamas is a prerequisite for a successful life? *(To Jesse.)* Do it because I'm your mother and I say so.

JESSE. No!

MAMA. Do it or no snack! *(To audience.)* He gets his pajamas on after doing a little dance in his underwear pretending to be a rapper … and checking off the date on his calendar and counting the days till Fourth of July … and playing earthquake … all of which I had to agree were more interesting than putting on pajamas. The part that troubles me is calling his father a fucking liar. *(Dad enters.)*

DAD. *(Wry.)* Well, he is in bed. And it's only ten-thirteen. What're all those books?

MAMA. Oh, I'm just doing a little reading on ADD.

DAD. *(Laughs.)* That teacher's full of shit, Jesse doesn't have ADD. He's just a boy! Can't a boy be a boy anymore, for chrissakes? I was the same when I was a kid. Worse. All the boys in my neighborhood were pretty wild. They stole. They tortured animals. They're cops and lawyers and businessmen now.

MAMA. Can I just read you a check list of symptoms of ADD?

DAD. Baby, please. I'd like a few minutes to relax, if you don't mind. *(He turns on the TV with the remote. We see and hear a blast of bombs go off on the news. Mama takes the remote and turns it off. She starts to read to him from the* DSM-IV, *a very thick book.)*

MAMA. These are the symptoms of Attention Deficit Disorder, according to the *DSM,* the manual psychiatrists use to diagnose. *(To audience.)* Oh, by the way, the proper name is now AD*H*D. The "H" stands for "Hyperactivity" — *(She is distracted by a blast of rap music from upstairs, possibly "Put On" or something equally raucous.*)

DAD. *(Yells.)* Turn it off! *(Jesse turns it down.)* Off! *(Jesse turns it low enough so Dad can't hear.)*

MAMA. *(Continuing to audience.)* Anyway, what was I saying? Oh — I'm just going to keep saying *ADD,* because that's what the comedians and the girl at the checkout counter say, as in — *(Valley girl space cadet.)* "Omigod, that was so ADD of me!" *(Reads.)* Symptoms of ADD: short attention span. Distractibility. Impulsivity. *(Dad impulsively grabs the remote and turns on the TV. Bush appears in close shots, as Mama continues.)* Lying. Blaming others for your mistakes … *(We continue to see Bush.)* Other symptoms include … poor judgment, trouble learning from experience, risk taking, and conflict seeking.

DAD. Okay, fine. Bush has ADD. Hey, at least it doesn't stop you from becoming president. But not our boy. Not Jesse.

MAMA. How can you be so sure?

DAD. Because those symptoms you read? Impulsivity, short attention span, risk taking — getting distracted? Those are symptoms — of childhood! Is childhood a disorder now?

MAMA. Of course not, but —

DAD. Besides … that thing the shrinks call "distractable"? What if that's the same thing, way back when, that made the hunter *aware* of

---

* See Special Note on Songs and Recordings on copyright page.

his environment, as in — *(Looking around; yells.)* "WHOA! WHAT'S THAT? TIGER? SHIT!" So instead of getting eaten, he brought home the bacon to the wife and kids. Or hey — what about the fireman who "risks" his life to run into a burning building? You really want to make him *sit down* at age six?

MAMA. You know what? Maybe you're right, honey.

DAD. You worry too much. *(He kisses her. But it's broken by a blast of loud rap. Dad storms upstairs.)* I'm coming up!

JESSE. *(Yells like a rapper.)* Scene Four!

Scene 4

Mama goes outside and jogs in place. A projection evoking the neighborhood appears.

MAMA. *(Jogging.)* The next morning, I go for a jog to keep my endorphins up and see my next-door neighbor eating a box of donuts in her car. I pretend not to notice because she's had a gastric bypass and I don't want to embarrass her ... but a moment later, she comes out. *(Sherry enters, wiping her mouth and hiding that donut.)*

SHERRY. Hi!

MAMA. Sherry, hi!

SHERRY. I saw Jesse out riding yesterday, he sure is getting fast on that bicycle!

MAMA. Uh-huh! How're Noah and Natalie?

SHERRY. Fabulous. Natalie's getting ready for her PSATs. And she's studying guitar! She's dying to babysit for you again.

MAMA. Great! We could use a night out!

SHERRY. And you got the invitation to Noah's bar mitzvah?

MAMA. We'll be there! Wow! He's learning all that Hebrew? That's amazing!

SHERRY. Well, he's on Ritalin now. *(Laughs.)* Without it, he couldn't get through *"Baruch atah adonai."*

MAMA. Who's he working with?

SHERRY. The rabbi or the psychiatrist?

MAMA. The psychiatrist?

SHERRY. David Jinks.

MAMA. *(Casually.)* Really? I think I've heard of him.

SHERRY. He's the best. But book him now if you're interested, because he books months in advance. So Jesse has ADD?

MAMA. *(Laughs.)* Oh — no! No, I mean we're just having him tested.

SHERRY. Well, Noah is doing really well! He was getting C's in all his classes. Couldn't concentrate. Bored stiff. Acting out, wearing black. This semester we started the Ritalin — he went up to an A-minus average. I'm really glad you're having Jesse tested early. Though you'll have to get him tested again by the school since he'll be getting disability status.

MAMA. *(Bit horrified.)* ADD is considered a … disability?

SHERRY. I know, I was a little put off too. But they'll have to give him special tutoring … extra time on tests … And, believe me, you'll be glad when the SATs roll around! Listen, I know people who actually try to get their kid labeled ADD so they'll have an advantage!

MAMA. Jeez! Well — like I said, we don't even know if he has it.

SHERRY. *(Knowing smile.)* Right.

MAMA. *(To audience.)* But I know what she's thinking —

SHERRY. *(To audience.)* Your kid is the poster child for ADD! He's a helluva lot more hyper than mine! He's a little menace to society on that bicycle. *(She turns back to Mama with a charming smile.)*

MAMA. But before I can make an excuse about having to — *(Remembers guiltily.)* work on that design plan … Our other neighbor comes out. *(Vera enters. She's a bit uptight. Maybe a bit flat. Utterly direct. And obsessive.)*

VERA. *(To Mama.)* Can Henry have a playdate with Jesse today?

MAMA. Gee, I'm afraid not, Vera.

VERA. How come?

MAMA. *(To audience.)* I want to say he's out of the country, but — *(To Vera.)* He has a special after-school class.

VERA. What's he taking?

MAMA. Magic.

VERA. Well, how about tomorrow? Henry's much better. He doesn't bite anymore.

MAMA and SHERRY. Great!

SHERRY. What's he taking now?

VERA. *(Proud.)* Just Zoloft.

SHERRY. Wow!

VERA. I'm sorry about your divorce.

SHERRY. *(Completely taken aback.)* Thank you ...

VERA. Are you selling the house?

SHERRY. No!

VERA. *(To Mama.)* Do you have the phone number of the people two doors down from you, by the way? Because they keep parking in front of my house, and I've left several notes on their car, and somebody just left a note on my car saying, "It's a free country" and I don't think that's very nice.

MAMA. I don't think I have their number.

VERA. Well, do you know their last names so I can look them up?

MAMA. Gee, I always just call them Brad and Bobby.

VERA. *(To Sherry.)* Do you know them?

SHERRY. I don't even know the people on my side. *(Vera continues gathering info, but you can't tell how she feels about what she's asking or how she registers the answers.)*

VERA. *(To Mama.)* Are they gay?

MAMA. I really couldn't say ...

VERA. Are they renting or do they own the house?

MAMA. Beats me ...

VERA. They're not lawyers, are they?

MAMA. I guess it's possible ...

VERA. Could you find out?

MAMA. I guess ... *(Vera has learned, in her own therapy, that the following is a good way to conclude a social interaction.)*

VERA. Okay, well ... Bye. *(She leaves.)*

MAMA and SHERRY. Bye-bye!

SHERRY. Boy, she's a little obsessive-compulsive, isn't she? I wonder if that's why her son has the anxiety disorder.

MAMA. There's a genetic connection?

SHERRY. *(Laughs.)* Please. Everything is genetic. Everything! *(Sherry leaves, finishing her donut.)*

Scene 5

MAMA. The next week I go see our doctor, Daniel Broder, who's known Jesse all his life. Daniel is not just an M.D., he's also a homeopath. Basically, the idea of homeopathy is that everyone has a certain remedy which is like a key — to you. And when you take this remedy — in the form of teeny tiny pills that taste, well, a lot like sugar, actually — then all the symptoms that are obscuring your true nature will fall away, and you will be … you. You will be well. Well — well for *you. (Daniel comes on. A fish tank or fountain is projected, establishing his office. Daniel and Mama hug. He has a firm, true hug that lasts a few beats longer than most.)*

DANIEL. So tell me, my friend, what's going on? *(He sits. Mama does too.)*

MAMA. Well, our psychologist's working hypothesis is anxiety. And, there's also been some mention of the, uh, possibility of ADD.

DANIEL. *(Laughs.)* Please, you should have seen me when I was a kid.

MAMA. You too?

DANIEL. They called me "Flash." I had two speeds — "fast" and "get the fuck out of my way!" I cut out sugar for the last thirty years, I'm fine.

MAMA. But I did get just a *little* concerned he might have ADD because I read the checklist in the *DSM* and I checked off the whole thing

DANIEL. Well, you know that the *DSM* broadened the definition for ADHD a few years back.

MAMA. Why? How do they do that?

DANIEL. *(Smiles.)* How do they do that? They hold a convention at a nice hotel … invite the top psychiatrists, propose a broader definition that includes more symptoms … and vote. The whole shebang was paid for by the drug company that makes Ritalin, by the way. Of course, a broader definition means they can diagnose — and medicate — more kids. And I'm sure the psychiatrists feel they're helping more kids. But let's see if we can find the right homeopathic remedy for Jesse instead.

MAMA. Great. That's exactly why I'm here.

DANIEL. How's his diet?

MAMA. Well, we tried taking him off wheat and dairy, like you told us. But it meant he couldn't have macaroni and cheese, or cookies at school, and that was making him kind of … anxious. And it was also kind of ruining my marriage.

DANIEL. Ruining your marriage?

MAMA. Well, you know how last time we were here my husband

said — *(Dad enters.)*

DAD. *(Warmly.)* Whatever we need to do to make Jesse's life a little easier, I'm all for it. If you say no wheat, no dairy, the least I can do is to give it a try. *(He exits.)*

DANIEL. Right.

MAMA. Well, when it came time for lunch, he was more, like — *(Dad reenters and declares ...)*

DAD. I'm having a pizza. No one is going to tell me what I can eat! Don't give me that spelt crap! Don't talk to me about soy cheese. I'm having a pizza, *goddamit! (He leaves.)*

MAMA. And of course Jesse wanted pizza too, so ...

DANIEL. Well, food is a very emotional issue for some people. Me, I'm good with a Boca Burger. And how's it going with the allergist?

MAMA. Oh — *(She calls offstage to her husband.)* Honey? *(Dad enters.)*

MAMA. Would you be the allergist for a sec — ?

DAD. No. *(He leaves.)*

ACTOR PLAYING DANIEL. Would you like me to be the allergist?

MAMA. Would you?

ACTOR PLAYING DANIEL. Sure — *(He picks up a chart and becomes the Allergist, all nose.)*

ALLERGIST. *(All stuffed up.)* Okay, let's see ... Last month, we scratch tested him for seventy-five different allergens and twenty-two foods ... And it seems he's allergic to ... dust.

DANIEL. Dust? Just dust?

ALLERGIST. *(Clears his clogged throat.)* That's it. *(He sits, becoming Daniel.)*

DANIEL. Alright. You know, even a food *sensitivity* — as opposed to an actual allergy — can affect behavior. So why don't you take him off wheat, dairy, and sugar again ... And I think I know the right remedy. *(He picks up a tiny jar from his desk and hands it to her.)* Give him half a capful of Nux Vomica for three days.

MAMA. Okay.

DANIEL. He may get worse for a while ...

MAMA. Uh-huh ...

DANIEL. But that's a sign that the Nux is working. You should see some results fairly soon.

MAMA. Oh good, because the school is getting pretty ... anxious.

DANIEL. You take good care. *(Daniel hugs Mama a beat too long and leaves.)*

MAMA. I start to drive home — *(Mama is in her car. Traffic sounds. Traffic on screen. Her cell rings.)* Hello? … Oh hi! … It's looking great! I'll have the designs and swatches for you tomorrow, and we can — *(Listens; reassuring.)* No, no, it'll be ready for your anniversary party, and it will be beautiful. *(She hears a beep for call waiting and sees the Caller I.D. Dad enters, in his car, on his cell. Into phone:)* Listen, the tile guy's on the other line, can I call you back? *(Switches calls.)* Hi honey, Daniel gave us a new homeo —

DAD. *(Into cell.)* Did you see the news?

MAMA. No. What happened? *(Mama finds a worn envelope that came out of her purse with the phone.)* Oh, here's that check for American Express — ! *(She swerves, nearly causing an accident.)*

DAD. There's a huge recall on peanut butter!

MAMA. Hold on, let me check it out — *(She checks the news on her cell as she drives. Sound of honking horns.)* Oh my God, I can't believe — *(A beep sounds.)*

DAD. Listen, I have another call. *(Another beep sounds.)*

MAMA. Oh — so do I.

DAD. I better take it, maybe it's the school. Jesse called Mrs. Holly's breasts "boobs" and he's in the principal's office.

MAMA. Why didn't you call me?

DAD. I am calling you.

MAMA. Why didn't *they* call me? *(Looks at phone.)* Oh. They did call. Fucking AT&T. Well, if it's the school, call me right back. And I'll call them. *(Both switch to other calls.)*

MAMA. Hello?

DAD. Hello? *(Dad's caller has hung up, so he does too. Mama talks to her caller.)*

MAMA. I'd love to donate to the Alumni Association, but I haven't lived up to my potential and I have no available cash. *(She ends the call. The kitchen returns.)*

Scene 6

JESSE'S VOICE. Scene Six!

MAMA. That night we start the homeopathic. *(Dad enters and puts bread in a frying pan.)*

DAD. I have no problem with homeopathy. If it'll help him to be a little calmer, I'm open-minded.

MAMA. Good. What are you making?

DAD. Grilled cheese.

MAMA. I'll make it for you, honey. Why don't you go up and get him into his pajamas.

DAD. All right. *(He leaves. Mama dumps the bread in the trash and puts another sandwich in the pan.)*

MAMA. I make it with spelt bread and soy cheese, and while I'm at it, I try to get in a little meditation. *(She meditates as she fries.)* "Lord make me an instrument of thy peace. Where there is hatred, let me sow love, where there is injury, pardon. Where there is doubt, faith — "*(Dad enters.)*

DAD. He's getting into his pajamas!

MAMA. You're kidding! *(To audience.)* We give the homeopathic three more weeks —

DAD. He's doing great!

MAMA. *(To audience.)* The next week he hits a boy in his class.

DAD. That kid is always cutting in front of him. That kid acts like a little goody two-shoes, but he's a real pain in the ass. *(Dad tastes Mama's sandwich and spits it out.)*

MAMA. Well, being a pain in the ass is not cause for suspension. And hitting is.

DAD. Well — boys hit!

MAMA. Our *boy* also rides his scooter straight out the driveway into traffic and has almost gotten himself hit — twice! I'm going back to Daniel. Maybe he needs to change the homeopathic.

DAD. Homeopathy is a bunch of crap.

MAMA. Well, what do you suggest? Our appointment with Dr. Waller isn't for another month.

DAD. You know what I suggest? Nothing. Leave the kid alone. Let him lead a normal life. *(Mrs. Holly enters.)*

MRS. HOLLY. I think the question is, is it normal for a child Jesse's age to be unable to sit through a ten-minute story? Is it normal for him to use four letter words before he can *spell?* Is it normal to collect endless bits and pieces of junk in his book bag — and forget to put in his homework assignment? And, if I put it in there *for* him — to forget to do it and bring it back? Because if you think that's normal, you are doing an enormous disservice to your child. Not to mention the twenty-seven other children in my class. *(Dad is fooling around, tapping with a utensil, or tossing and catching an apple.)* Are you listening to me?

DAD. Sorry. I was just …

MRS. HOLLY. Well, sit down. *(He sits, fast. To Mama.)* Now where are we?

MAMA. *(To audience.)* Luckily, Dr. Waller has a cancellation, so —

DAD. Lucky us!

MAMA. *(To Holly.)* We're having him tested.

MRS. HOLLY. Good. *(Leaves, muttering.)* Since you won't listen to someone who's been teaching twenty-two years …

MAMA. Dr. Waller spends two entire days testing Jesse, and we go to her office for the results.

Scene 7

JESSE. Yo! Scene Seven! *(Mama and Dad sit down in Dr. Waller's waiting room. The screen changes to another Impressionist painting.)*

MAMA. Isn't that the same painting that's in Dr. Zavala's waiting room?

DAD. I don't know. I never noticed.

MAMA. What is it with psychotherapists and Impressionists?

DAD. I don't know. Don't you have to ring a bell or something? *(Dr. Waller enters.)*

DR. WALLER. I thought you might be waiting! Why don't you step into my office? *(A different Impressionist print appears and Mama and Dad sit down in her office. Dr. Waller consults a computer or pad with her notes.)* Well, first of all, I want to say that Jesse did an amazing job on my tests.

MAMA. *(Thrilled.)* Really?

DAD. See!

DR. WALLER. Two full days of testing is quite a lot for any little boy, but he really stuck with it like a champ. We took a lot of breaks, of course. We went downstairs and played in the fountain. Took a ride around the parking lot. Played games … Ran up and down the stairs … Several times … *(Laughs.)* He certainly is a very energetic child!

DAD. Well, he's a boy …

DR. WALLER. He sure is! So first let me tell you about his strengths.

MAMA. Good! *(Dad squirms a lot during the following.)*

DR. WALLER. His verbal skills are in the superior range. Fine and gross motor skills are superior as well. That boy can run! Visuoperception and visuomotor integration are in the high average range.

MAMA. Great! *(Dad's cell phone rings.)*

DAD. Sorry, I won't — *(He declines the call.)*

DR. WALLER. His ability to remember what he's read is in the average range.

MAMA. *(To audience.)* "Average" is such a sad word nowadays.

DR. WALLER. As are his learning and memory for spatial information and visual details. *(Dad's foot starts to shake.)*

MAMA. *(Continuing to audience.)* Everything's got to be "excellent"!

DR. WALLER. But I suspect that may be more attentional than —

MAMA. *(Continuing to audience.)* "Excellent" is the new "Good."

DR. WALLER. *(Trying to get Mama's attention.)* In fact, I think most of his difficulties have an attentional component — *(Dad's voice mail rings. He shuts off the phone.)*

DAD. Sorry. So he has no learning disabilities?

DR. WALLER. Oh no —

DAD. *(To Mama.)* See?

DR. WALLER. His problems are more with focusing long enough to —

MAMA. What about an anxiety disorder?

DR. WALLER. He can be very anxious, but that would not be my primary diagnosis.

DAD. And what would that be?

DR. WALLER. Well, as I said, his difficulties are *attentional* … So I'd say Attention Deficit Hyperactivity Disorder. *(Silence. Dad's foot shakes. Dr. Waller notices. Finally —)*

MAMA. I see.

DR. WALLER. Studies indicate the best course of treatment is a combination of behavior modification and medication — *(Dad gets up.)*

DAD. Thank you.

MAMA. My husband is late for an appointment.

DR. WALLER. *(Smiles; to audience.)* Well, we all know that's a big lie.

MAMA. *(To audience.)* She didn't say that, of course. *(Dr. Waller crosses to Mama and hands her a paper.)*

DR. WALLER. I've jotted down the names of a few very fine child psychiatrists. *(Truly.)* It was a pleasure working with your family. Call me anytime.

MAMA. Thanks. *(Mama follows Dad, who's already outside. Dr. Waller hurries offstage, possibly because she's starting to cry.)*

DAD. *(Upset.)* Listen, I have to get back to work. Can we talk about all this tonight?

MAMA. All right ... *(He leaves. Mama is left with the audience.)* Well ... at least we've got a diagnosis ... Then again, as Jesse would say — *(A pained laugh.)* Well — duh! I mean, I knew something was up before he was *born* for chrissakes! He was doing karate in my belly. And when he popped out, he just had this look in his eye like — "Let's get this party started, Mama!" I mean — he never took a nap, never slept through the night in his life — *(Fighting tears.)* He's — the most interesting person I've ever met. He makes up knock-knock jokes. Invents hors d'oeuvres. He collects anything that lights up, anything that explodes ... He raps — *(Mrs. Holly comes on.)*

MRS. HOLLY. *(Kindly.)* But he cannot — *cannot* — stay on task. You know, Thomas Edison Elementary has the best test scores in the city —

MAMA. But Thomas Edison never would have made it through Thomas Edison — because Thomas Edison had ADD! You know, some amazing people have had ADD. Mozart had it, Einstein ... Tom Sawyer, Huck Finn ...

MRS. HOLLY. Mrs. Cara. A child with ADD is going to have trouble paying attention in *any* educational setting. How's he going to get through the next ten years?

MAMA. *(After a beat.)* I don't know, Mrs. Holly.

MRS. HOLLY. Well, the sign of intelligence is not *having* the answers but, rather, knowing where to go to find them. *(Mrs. Holly looks at the paper in Mama's hands and exits. Mama puts the paper in her pocket.)*

JESSE. Scene Eight!

MAMA. That night is our date night, and Sherry's daughter Natalie comes to babysit. *(Hip hop music, something like "Low," begins. Natalie runs on, out of breath and a bit manic.*)*

NATALIE. Sorry I'm late! *(A lie.)* I was studying for my calculus test and it was really interesting and I was really into it and I guess I kind of just got lost in the whole track of time thing. You can stay out later if you want. Don't worry about me. Stay out till eleven, twelve — one, two, whatever.

JESSE. *(Excited.)* Scene Eight!

MAMA. Okay, well, you have our cells. No rap, and try to get him to bed by nine-thirty —

JESSE. Scene Eight, woman!

NATALIE. Oh, no problem, we always find good stuff to do! Have a good time!

Scene 8

JESSE. *(Excited.)* Scene Eight! *(Car alarm sound.)* ENH-ENH-ENH-WOO-OO-WOO-OO-ENH-ENH-ENH *(Dad turns off Jesse's alarm with his remote. Disarming alarm:)* Beep-beep.

MAMA. I let my husband choose the violent action-adventure movie. *(They sit. We see two seconds of a violent movie on screen.)* After, we go out to eat and to talk. *(They rise. A sports bar is projected. Games on screen. They sit at a table. Dad is completely distracted by the game. After a few beats, Mama asks ...)* Do you have to?

DAD. Sorry. What are you having?

MAMA. Chicken Caesar. You?

DAD. Fettuccini Alfredo. *(A game continues in the background, but it should be slow enough not to distract us from the scene.)*

MAMA. So, I think we need to talk about Dr. Waller. *(A Waitress arrives. She, too, is distracted by the game on screen.)*

WAITRESS. Would you care for something to drink? Some wine? Or beer?

---

* See Special Note on Songs and Recordings on copyright page.

DAD. Two red wines.

WAITRESS. *(Watching the TV.)* Bottle or draft?

MAMA. We'll just have two glasses of red wine.

WAITRESS. Thank you. *(The Waitress leaves. Freeze the game if it's distracting.)*

MAMA. *(To audience.)* Then I notice Daniel, sitting all alone, and invite him to join us.

DAD. What the hell for?

MAMA. Because he's sitting all by himself! And maybe I can get some advice without paying for an office visit. *(Daniel enters and joins them with his salad and water.)*

DANIEL. Thanks, guys! Good to see you! *(To Dad.)* Good to see *you,* my friend! *(Daniel bends down and gives Dad a big hug. The Waitress brings two wines.)*

MAMA. *(To Daniel.)* Would you like a glass of wine?

DANIEL. I don't do well with the sulfites.

DAD. Too bad.

MAMA. *(Very casually.)* So, tell me, Daniel, is it me, or is there just a helluva lot of ADD going around?

DANIEL. *(Laughs.)* Please. Half my practice! *(Daniel pours a powdered vitamin packet into his water.)*

MAMA. So why *is* there so much more ADD nowadays?

DANIEL. Jesus. Where to begin? Do you have a garden?

DAD. Of course.

DANIEL. Use any pesticides?

DAD. If we want stuff like flowers and grass … *(Daniel launches in, passionate about this stuff.)*

DANIEL. Well, did you know that monkeys develop ADD-like symptoms when they're around pesticides? Rats become aggressive, impulsive …

DAD. I'm curious. How do they measure impulsiveness in rats?

DANIEL. They bite more.

DAD. And how do you know that's impulsive and not thought out? Maybe they're pissed off about being tested all the time and treated like … rats.

MAMA. Honey. Go on, Daniel. I had no idea!

DANIEL. DDT and dioxin also cause hyperactivity in mice.

DAD. But aren't all mice hyper? Isn't that sort of their thing? They scurry. I mean, if a mouse were laid-back, wouldn't *that* be considered a problem?

DANIEL. Right on. *(The Waitress returns with food.)*

WAITRESS. *(Confused.)* I hope this is your order ... Two more wines? *(She gives Dad Mama's order and vice versa, so they switch plates.)*

DAD. Bring a bottle. *(The Waitress nods and leaves.)*

MAMA. *(Laughs.)* So, if we just stay out of the garden ...

DANIEL. *(Smiles.)* I'm afraid there's a shitload of hazardous chemicals inside your house too. In your carpet, the particle board in your bookcase, your mattress ... Formaldehyde, benzene, toluene ... And all these can affect learning, memory — *(Smiles at Dad.)* and mood. *(Dad starts to eat.)*

MAMA. *(Jokes.)* So, maybe we have to build a new house! What else?

DANIEL. Well — food, of course.

DAD. *(Eating.)* Of course ...

DANIEL. Our food is processed with thousands of additives, not to mention the dyes that are in everything from Jell-O to Children's Tylenol. I'm telling you, man, food colorings can make a kid want to buy a trench coat and shoot up his freshman class.

MAMA. *(Laughs.)* So, food's out. Anything else?

DANIEL. Well, even the car can be a problem. There's often mold in the upholstery, PCBs emitted by the air conditioner —

DAD. Guess I won't be driving the kid to school ...

DANIEL. *(Smiles.)* Hey, might not be a bad idea, considering the asbestos and lead paint in some schools. *(Dad's phone rings. The ringtone is Jesse's hip hop. Dad answers.)*

DAD. Excuse me. *(Into phone.)* Hi, Jess, what's up? ... Well, you have to put them on ... Jesse — I don't want to hear that language, you hear me? Especially not about Natalie ... Because it's not nice to talk about people's bodies. *(The Waitress brings a bottle of wine, shows it to Dad, and struggles to get it open. It takes a while.)*

MAMA. Tell him all bodies are beautiful. *(The Waitress chuckles.)*

DAD. *(Into phone.)* All bodies are beautiful, even fat ones. So put on the pj's or no Wii for the rest of the weekend. Bye, honey. Love you. *(A loud cheer.)* Oombagga, oombagga, oombagga, oom! *(Ends call; to Daniel.)* Sorry, did I miss anything? *(Daniel launches right back in. The Waitress is still struggling with the bottle, which is now between her legs for leverage.)*

DANIEL. Well — the air, of course. Mold, pollen, exhaust fumes, all can affect learning — *(Glances at Dad.)* and mood. Clearly, kids in the poorer parts of town have it the worst. And I don't even want to get into radiation —

DAD. Good.

DANIEL. But since nuclear testing began in the fifties — *(Dad is wolfing down his meal. The waitress finally has the bottle open and starts to pour, in her own distracted way.)*

DAD. Anything else?

DANIEL. Well, this is controversial, guys. But the rise in the use of vaccines directly parallels the rise in the incidence of both autism and ADD. Until recently there was a mercury preservative used in vaccines called thimerosal. Mercury is a known neurotoxin — so all our kids got it in all their vaccines!

DAD and MAMA. What! *(The Waitress is still pouring distractedly.)*

DAD. Can we get a check? *(The Waitress leaves. Mama, almost giddy with information, slowly downs another entire glass of wine before she speaks.)*

MAMA. So. Basically, what you're saying ... is that our house, garden, car, school, air, food — and/or vaccines — could be giving Jesse ADD!?

DANIEL. *(Chewing.)* Or, hey, it could be genetic ... *(The Waitress returns and hands Dad the check.)*

WAITRESS. I didn't charge you for the beer.

DAD. Thank you very much.

DANIEL. How much do I owe for the salad?

MAMA. Oh, nothing, it's our pleasure.

DAD. Thirteen sixty-three with the tax.

DANIEL. *(Pleasantly.)* Here you go. *(He hands Dad a bill and rises.)* 'Night now! Be well! *(Hugs Mama.)* Enjoy your evening! *(He leaves.)*

MAMA. I cannot believe you let him pay for the salad.

DAD. Believe it, baby.

MAMA. How could you do that?

DAD. Because he ruined my dinner! Why the hell do you think he was eating alone!? Homeopathy. Teeny tiny little pills ... Pussy medicine. Let's just go home. *(The restaurant changes to their bedroom. Natalie runs on wearing a different T-shirt.)*

Scene 9

JESSE. Scene Nine!

NATALIE. He's sleeping!

MAMA. How'd it go?

NATALIE. It was great! It was awesome! We crashed cars, made hors d'oeuvres, set off stink bombs ... We did magic, watched Disney, went biking, played Wii ...

DAD. *(Hands her some bills.)* Glad somebody had a good evening. Here you go.

NATALIE. Thanks. Call me anytime! Even a weeknight, Monday, Tuesday, Wednesday ... whatever.

MAMA. Say hi to your mom! *(Natalie makes a face or a grunt about her mom as she leaves.)*

DAD. The one night a week we get to go out. Our date night. I don't even feel like watching the news. Let's just go to bed. *(A bed comes on ... or just pillows. They sit.)*

MAMA. *(To audience.)* We start to make love. *(They kiss. To audience.)* Because it's our date night. *(They resume the kiss. Her cell phone rings, Jesse's ring tone. She breaks the kiss and answers.)* Jesse — Jesse, stop crying, sweetie. We didn't want to wake you! We're right in the next room ... Jesse — don't call me a liar. I swear to you, I'll knock on the wall —

JESSE. *(Desperately.)* MOOOOM!

DAD. Go. *(Mama rises.)*

MAMA. *(To audience.)* I return in less than an hour. *(Mama lies down and they start to make love. She stops.)* I'm so sorry. I can't.

DAD. *(Sits up.)* Why not? Is sex toxic?

MAMA. I'm sorry, I'm just not in the mood.

DAD. I'm not in the mood either! Should that stop us? On our date night?! This is exactly why I let him pay for the damn salad.

MAMA. I know. I feel terrible. Do you want a blow job?

DAD. *(With sudden emotion.)* No, I don't want a blow job! I want a life! I want a life free of doctors and shrinks and neuropsychologists and homeopaths! I want to eat without fear! I want to take my kid to school and know that he'll *be* there till three o'clock, and not get sent home at twelve. He's nine years old — just once I want

36

him to sleep through the night! I want him to play Little League without freaking out because the other kids are gonna "watch him bat." I want — a normal child! *(They are both horrified by what he's said. After several beats ...)* All right. I'll settle for the blow job. *(Mama starts to turn to him. Then —)*
JESSE. Mooom!

Scene 10

JESSE. Scene Whatever! *(The bedroom changes to the kitchen, as they continue.)*
MAMA. Time for school, Jesse!
JESSE. Time for school, Jesse!
MAMA. Don't imitate me.
JESSE. Don't imitate me.
MAMA. It's disrespectful!
JESSE. It's disrespectful!
MAMA. And I want it to stop!
JESSE. And I want it to stop! *(Mama takes a breath.)*
MAMA. *(Calmly.)* If you stop, you may play your Wii tonight.
JESSE. If you stop, you may play your Wii tonight.
MAMA. Okay, no Wii.
JESSE. Yes, Wii! *(Imitating Dad now.)* Can't a boy be a boy, for crissakes?
MAMA. I am serious here, Jesse.
JESSE. I am serious here, Jesse.
MAMA. You'd better be dressed!
JESSE. You'd better be dressed!
MAMA. It goes back and forth like this till one of us loses it and says — *(To Jesse; raw.)* SHUT UP! JUST SHUT UP AND PUT YOUR CLOTHES ON!
JESSE. YOU SHUT UP! I HATE YOU! YOU'RE RUINING MY FUCKING LIFE!
MAMA. *(Screams.)* YOU'RE RUINING MY FUCKING LIFE TOO! *(Long beat; to audience.)* Of course, I didn't say that, but, to my horror ... I thought it.

Scene 11

JESSE. Scene Eleven! Shit!! *(Mama's desk wheels on or the counter turns into her desk. She gets her design portfolio, swatches, and fringe.)*
MAMA. *(Angry and determined.)* I sit down to do some work for my client! Because I am a professional. And I love my work. And I always fulfill my commitments on time. And I can make a simple decision about fringe. *(She goes to get coffee.)* But when I go to the kitchen for coffee ... I see a long sleeved T-shirt in the wastebasket with blood on the sleeves ... *(Takes T-shirt.)* And hear Natalie practicing the guitar in her garage. *(We hear Natalie on electric guitar.)*
NATALIE. *(Offstage; singing, screeching.)* This is my life! Your life is over! This is my life! Your life is over!
MAMA. She reminds me of me trying to meditate. I invite her over and make her a peanut butter sandwich, as I've done since she was seven when we moved here so Jesse could grow up in a good neighborhood. *(Natalie enters, and Mama hands her a sandwich.)* So how's it going, Natalie?
NATALIE. Oh, you know ...
MAMA. Your mom says you're studying for your PSATs?
NATALIE. *(Laughs.)* Sort of!
MAMA. And you're playing the guitar!
NATALIE. Yeah, I'm trying to put together a garage band.
MAMA. Cool.
NATALIE. Jesse wants to be in it. I gave him a CD of Linkin Park, he really loves it, and I figured he wouldn't understand the bad words.
MAMA. Uh-huh ...
NATALIE. He is exactly like me when I was a kid! *(Natalie notices Mama's designs.)* What's this?
MAMA. Oh, something I'm working on for a client. That's the dining room. *(Natalie plays with a piece of fringe.)*
NATALIE. You have such a cool job. Like playing house.
MAMA. Well, I do love helping people live in a beautiful home. I mean — not that beauty solves anything. But it helps to sit down and face things in a well-designed chair. *(To audience.)* There is simply no good way to do this — *(To Natalie.)* So, Natalie, I found this T-shirt with blood on the sleeves in my wastebasket.

NATALIE. *(Grabs T-shirt.)* Oh shit, I meant to take that with me and I forgot. Please don't tell my mom I was cutting, she gets so freaked out.

MAMA. You're cutting?

NATALIE. I only do it on my arm …

MAMA. With … what?

NATALIE. Just a razor …

MAMA. *(To audience.)* I want to say, "MY RAZOR!?" But I know that wouldn't sound right.

NATALIE. It's no big deal, a lot of kids do it.

MAMA. But … Why?

NATALIE. I don't know, I just get kind of uptight sometimes? And I feel like I've got to do it? And I know I shouldn't … But I've just got to?

MAMA. Like … masturbating?

NATALIE. Please. I would *so* not do that. That's gross.

MAMA. But — doesn't it hurt?

NATALIE. *(Shrugs.)* I just kind of feel kind of … numb? And then after I do it, I feel normal again.

MAMA. And then it … heals?

NATALIE. Uh-huh. And when you pick off the scabs — it's like you get to do it all over again. Like — you take a piece of yourself off. Like … shedding? Anyway. Listen, I've gotta go. I've got a guitar lesson … *(Natalie picks up her guitar. She has the guitar in one hand, the T-shirt in the other. Mama reaches for the T-shirt.)*

MAMA. Can I take that for you?

NATALIE. That's okay. Thanks for the sandwich — *(She starts to leave. Mama follows her outside.)*

MAMA. Oh, no problem. *(Natalie exits. Mama follows, looking after her.)*

NATALIE. *(Offstage.)* Call me if you need me to babysit!

MAMA. I will …

Scene 12

The neighborhood is projected on screen. Vera enters.

VERA. Oh, hi. Can Henry have a playdate with Jesse today?

MAMA. I don't think so, Vera.

VERA. Why not?

MAMA. Because … Frankly, Vera, Jesse's having some issues.

VERA. Who is he seeing?

MAMA. No one. He's not seeing anyone.

VERA. We see David Jinks.

MAMA. You do?

VERA. He's very good. He listens.

MAMA. And he's helpful?

VERA. He got Henry off Prozac, which was making him have tics, and put him on Zoloft. And he put me on Prozac — which is helping me a lot.

MAMA. *(To audience.)* I know this is a terrible thing to ask, but Vera is not one to stand on ceremony, so — *(To Vera.)* May I ask why you take Prozac?

VERA. Well, you know I'm obsessive-compulsive.

MAMA. Really?

VERA. You've been to my house. You know I can't stand it when you put a cup down. Listen, I'm sorry Jesse is having a hard time. If you ever want to talk … You know, most mothers don't really understand.

MAMA. Well thanks, Vera.

VERA. Or if you want to rent a movie sometime …

MAMA. Thanks.

VERA. You should go to Curves with me. There's fifteen machines and you change every thirty seconds so you never get bored.

MAMA. Wow —

VERA. I like your shoes. Have you ever bought shoes on the Internet?

MAMA. No.

VERA. I've just started buying them from Zappos.com. I get a little overwhelmed in malls. Especially with the terrorists and all. And even if you can't afford a mortgage anymore, you can always buy shoes. Zappos has pictures of thousands and thousands of shoes, and they send them to you in like three days, and if they don't work out, you just send them back free of charge. It's fun!

MAMA. Really? Well — thanks.

VERA. Okay … bye. *(Vera exits.)*

MAMA. *(To audience.)* I forget about walking. I go online and find Zappos.com. *(She goes to her computer. She touches a few keys and hundreds of pictures of shoes are projected and scroll down the screen.)* I search the selections for about an hour and buy seven pairs because it's a lot more fun than — well, my life. While I'm on the 'Net, I google ADD. *(Hundreds of ADD sites scroll down the screen.)* There are a million sites. More sites than there are shoes on Zappos. I call Dr. Zavala. *(Dr. Zavala comes on, on a cell.)*

DR. ZAVALA. You sound very upset. I have a cancellation at two —

MAMA. Oh! Did someone get better?

DR. ZAVALA. What — ? Oh! Glad to see you're keeping your sense of humor. Why don't you come in?

MAMA. All right. *(The kitchen disappears. Dr. Zavala and Mama sit, as Zavala's print appears.)*

DR. ZAVALA. Have you thought about calling a psychiatrist?

MAMA. I don't need a psychiatrist! What I need is to finish one lousy dining room — make a simple decision about fringe! —

DR. ZAVALA. I meant for Jesse.

MAMA. Look, I know what a psychiatrist does — a psychiatrist prescribes drugs. For a nine-year-old child!

DR. ZAVALA. I understand. I think you're right to try everything else first, every conceivable good option.

MAMA. *(Eagerly.)* Good, like neurofeedback? Orthomolecular therapy? Herbs?

DR. ZAVALA. I'm afraid the research on alternative methods is purely anecdotal.

MAMA. *(To audience.)* Why is it that when a doctor says "anecdotal" it sounds like another word for "bullshit"?

DR. ZAVALA. *(Hurt.)* I'm here to help you. I made time to see you today.

MAMA. Sorry. So what other conceivable good option can we try?

DR. ZAVALA. Well, a good behavior-modification program is essential, with or without medication.

MAMA. Okay. That's what Doctor Waller recommended too! Let's do it.

DR. ZAVALA. Terrific. Well, first … You're going to buy a set of poker chips.

MAMA. Poker chips?

DR. ZAVALA. Yes. *(Dr. Zavala delineates the program with great enthusiasm.)* Then you're going to make a chart of all the behaviors you want to see from Jesse. So for instance: If he gets into pajamas on the first request — you'll give him five poker chips. If he doesn't … you'll *take away* five poker chips as a consequence. Then you'll ask his teacher to make a list of behaviors *she* wants to see … And you'll make two more charts — for Rewards. Daily Rewards might be watching TV, having dessert, riding his bike … And Future Rewards are special events — like a movie — or a shopping spree for something he really wants — *(Dying for one.)* like a new iPod Touch, say, with Safari — YouTube — Accelerometer — and Shazam!

MAMA. But shouldn't there be some perks that just come with childhood?

DR. ZAVALA. Unfortunately, it's not easy to motivate the ADHD child to comply, and that's causing enormous difficulties … So maybe the question you need to ask is, "Is Jesse enjoying his childhood?"

MAMA. *(After a beat.)* I'll give the chips a try.

DR. ZAVALA. Terrific. Shall we make an appointment for next week to see how it's going?

MAMA. Sure. *(To audience.)* Why even get up? *(They don't.)*

DR. ZAVALA. *(Brightly.)* So how's it going?

MAMA. Oh, wait — *(To audience; excited.)* Seven pairs of shoes arrived from Zappos.com. *(A UPS person, played by the actress who plays Holly comes on with a big Zappos carton. She plops it down and starts to leave.)* None fit. I sent them back — *(The UPS person picks up the carton and starts to leave.)* And ordered seven more. *(The UPS person drops the carton, with attitude, and leaves.)*

DR. ZAVALA. So! How's it going?

MAMA. Well, my husband said it wasn't fair that Jesse had to earn points to ride his bike, because exercise is necessary for a child. He also said Jesse should get some warnings before losing points — *(Dad comes on.)*

DAD. He also said he knew an excellent place to *put* the poker chips! *(He gives a thumbs up and leaves.)*

DR. ZAVALA. *(Annoyed.)* Well, it is essential that both parents be on the same page —

MAMA. *(To audience.)* I think she's getting annoyed with me —

DR. ZAVALA. *(Defensive.)* I am not getting annoyed! I'm trying to help you!

MAMA. And it's very hard on Jesse …

JESSE. I'm the only kid in the world who has to have poker chips to watch *SpongeBob*! You don't have to have poker chips to watch CNN!

MAMA. And Jesse's teacher is not cooperating at all —

DR. ZAVALA. Then maybe the three of us should meet at school. *(Mrs. Holly enters. The Impressionist print minimizes and the blackboard takes its place.)*

MRS. HOLLY. *(Resentful.)* He forgets to give me the Daily Rewards sheet so I can fill it out and give him his chips. And when he remembers, he forgets to bring it home.

DR. ZAVALA. Well, I can certainly understand your frustration —

MAMA. *(To audience.)* But if he could remember the Daily Rewards Sheet, he wouldn't need the Daily Rewards Sheet because he wouldn't have ADD!

MRS. HOLLY. I heard that! You know, the other mothers are whispering about you.

MAMA. *(To Zavala.)* I don't know if she actually said that —

DR. ZAVALA. But it's certainly how you *feel* —

MAMA. Yes! The minute I walk in her classroom, *I* feel like a child again!

DR. ZAVALA. Well, parents are allowed to have their feelings too —

MRS. HOLLY. What about the teacher? Is she allowed to have any feelings?

DR. ZAVALA. Of course!

MRS. HOLLY. Is she a human being?

DR. ZAVALA. Absolutely!

MRS. HOLLY. Do you think she does it for the *money?* In this town?

DR. ZAVALA. Of course not! Didn't I just acknowledge — twice — ?

MRS. HOLLY. *(Emotional.)* I went into this job because I love learning. And I want to give that to my kids. I loved school! School was the one place that made sense. Where two and two made four! Where you knew you'd have Pledge of Allegiance — and *then*

43

Science — and *then* P.E. — and *then* Math and Recess — because it was right up there on the board. You could count on it. And if you did your job in third grade, little lady, you got to fourth. Ulysses S. Grant Elementary. Where a good girl could read a good book and wind up in a castle — *(Carried away.)* and get away from her crazy alcoholic mother for seven whole hours!

DR. ZAVALA. Look. I think we're all here because we care. About Jesse. So how about this. Could you *ask* him for the Daily Rewards Sheet and fill it out and put it in his book bag?

MAMA. Could you please just try that?

MRS. HOLLY. If I didn't have twenty-seven other children in my class, I could! And I could follow him into the bathroom so he doesn't get into wet paper towel fights! And while I'm there, maybe even help him wipe his little —

MAMA. *(To audience.)* You know she didn't say that. But what she did say was much worse.

MRS. HOLLY. I'm going to recommend he be sent to special ed.

MAMA. But according to Dr. Waller's report, he has no learning disabilities!

MRS. HOLLY. Maybe not. But my entire *class* is learning-disabled when he's there. *(She exits, as Dad enters, joining Mama in Dr. Zavala's office. The Impressionist print replaces the blackboard.)*

DR. ZAVALA. *(Heartfelt.)* Clearly we are at a crisis point … where Jesse's self-esteem is at stake. Where Jesse himself must be feeling that something is very wrong. So what I am going to say … *(To Mama.)* And you know I don't say this lightly … *(To both.)* But we've tried a number of approaches … From behavior modification — to homeopathy! And at this point, I'd be terribly negligent if I did *not* say …

MAMA. *(To audience.)* Is there some way to not have to hear this!?

DR. ZAVALA. Ritalin.

DAD. Ritalin.

MAMA. *(After a beat; to Zavala.)* Tell me … What kind of a parent drugs a nine-year-old?

DR. ZAVALA. One who leaves no stone unturned when she's trying to help her child.

DAD. Well. *(Beat.)* Thanks for your opinion. *(To Mama.)* Let's go.

MAMA. Hold on … I'm thinking … I'm trying to —

DAD. What's to think about?! Let's go. *(A pause as Mama searches for questions …)*

MAMA. *(To Zavala.)* Would Ritalin … get him out of his pajamas?

DR. ZAVALA. When Ritalin works, it can seem like a miracle.

DAD. I am not putting my kid on Ritalin!

MAMA. *(To Dad.)* Would Ritalin … get him a friend to sit with at lunch?

DAD. No way am I putting my kid on Ritalin! *(A beat. When Mama speaks, it's more to herself than to them.)*

MAMA. *(Fighting tears.)* Would Ritalin be a better mother than I am? *(Dad stares at Mama.)*

End of Act One

ACT TWO

Scene 13

Van Gogh's self-portrait with pipe is on screen. Mama enters from one side of the stage, Dr. Jinks from the other.

DR. JINKS. Dr. David Jinks. Please — sit. *(Mama sits.)* Giving a child with ADHD Ritalin is like giving a child with diabetes insulin. Or giving a child with astigmatism glasses. The world comes into focus for the first time. Before Ritalin, you can give a child the same instruction day in, day out, and no matter how clear you are, how strict you are, what a good parent you are ... it may simply not stick. You tell the child to "pay attention" — he may simply have no concept of what you're talking about. With Ritalin, he simply cannot *not* pay attention.

MAMA. Why? What does it do?

DR. JINKS. It's a stimulant. Which the ADD brain needs. ADD occurs as a result of neurological dysfunction in the prefrontal cortex of the brain, which is like the "executive control center" —

MAMA. "*Executive* control center"? Like — the government of the brain?

DR. JINKS. Excellent analogy. Now, interestingly, when people with ADD try to concentrate, prefrontal cortex activity actually decreases rather than increases, which is why so many people with ADD unconsciously seek conflict or even crisis as a way to stimulate their own prefrontal cortex. Or they engage in high risk activities —

MAMA. *(To audience.)* Like — war?

DR. JINKS. Are you with me? Am I going too fast?

MAMA. Not at all. *(He begins to speak louder, more insistently, his voice miked ... or so it seems to her.)*

DR. JINKS. ADD is a life-span disorder. Thirty-five percent of kids with ADD never finish high school. Forty-five percent of males with ADD are arrested for a felony before the age of sixteen,

46

and fifty to seventy-five percent of the prison population has some form of ADD. The divorce rate for people with ADD is two times the average, they're five times as likely to get into car accidents —

MAMA. *(To audience.)* He's probably saying all this quite calmly —

DR. JINKS. *(Sits; calmly.)* And people with untreated ADD are three times more likely to abuse drugs.

MAMA. And by "untreated" you mean — ?

DR. JINKS. Unmedicated.

MAMA. So, if my son takes a drug, he's less likely to take … drugs?

DR. JINKS. He is less likely to self-medicate, yes.

MAMA. But isn't Ritalin a Class 2 restricted drug for its potential for addiction and abuse? Isn't it speed?

DR. JINKS. As I said, it is a stimulant. Methylphenidate. Other medications for ADD such as Adderall are Amphetamines.

MAMA. And these drugs — sorry, medications — can cure ADD?

DR. JINKS. The patient is able to concentrate while the drug is active in the system.

MAMA. And when it wears off?

DR. JINKS. He is himself again.

MAMA. Oh terrific. So Ritalin doesn't cure? You can take it for the rest of your life and it doesn't cure a fucking thing?

ACTOR PLAYING JINKS. *(Gets up.)* Whoa, whoa. I got to stop. *(To the stage manager.)* I got to stop. *(To Mama.)* You think I would even remember my fucking lines if it weren't for Ritalin? No less be able to memorize four different parts!?

MAMA. You have ADD? I never —

ACTOR. Because I'm on Ritalin! Well, Adderal now. Look. I could memorize the phone book on Ritalin! I could clean my apartment and yours — *(To audience member.)* and yours too! Because what Ritalin does is allow a person to stay on task — as I'm doing right now — instead of flying off on a million little tangents — *(To Mama.)* Like, oh, some people. It allows a kid to have a shot at forming habits which he might even be able to keep up without the drug — medication — so that someday he might even be able to get a PhD and help others! Or *play* a person with a PhD who helps others!

MAMA. Okay, *Dr. Jinks,* but if van Gogh had been on Ritalin, would he have done that painting? *(Mama points to the screen.)*

DR. JINKS. *(Sits.)* Some of my patients do experience a decrease

47

in creativity. *(As Actor.)* But, hey, you know what? If van Gogh had taken Ritalin, he might not have cut off his goddamn ear!

MAMA. Is it safe?

DR. JINKS. They've been using Ritalin for fifty years. It is the most studied of all drugs for children.

MAMA. What about side effects?

DR. JINKS. The most common are loss of appetite, delayed growth, and insomnia, but we can always add another drug like Clonidine to help the insomnia. Some children develop tics, but we can add a little Tenex to control that.

MAMA. But if it's a real disease — like diabetes — then shouldn't one thing work. Like insulin. Why is there a "checklist of symptoms," which puts the diagnosis in the hands of the checker ... instead of a real, objective test?

DR. JINKS. The brain is highly complex, Mrs. Cara. I believe I said earlier — *(As Actor.)* Maybe you missed it — *(As Jinks.)* That ADD is a neurological condition. An *hereditary* condition. *(He notices his light is on.)* Would you excuse me a moment? I don't know why my light is on. My next appointment must have gotten confused and come a little early. Let me just go see. *(He exits.)*

MAMA. And while he's gone, I leave through the other door. So I can be home before my husband. *(The Van Gogh disappears. Jesse's self-portrait fills the screen. A couch might come on. Dad's there.)*

DAD. So you want to put Jesse on drugs.

MAMA. *(Quietly.)* No.

DAD. So what'd you see a psychiatrist for?

MAMA. Information ...

DAD. I see. Just doing your homework?

MAMA. Just ... trying to keep an open mind.

DAD. 'Cause, see, where I come from? "Drugs" is kind of a bad word. Like — if they sell it on the street, I don't want my kid getting it from the school nurse. *(Ironic but deadly.)* Know what I'm sayin'?

MAMA. Yes I do.

DAD. I also have a little problem with the idea of somebody giving my son drugs to keep him nice and quiet. Maybe I don't think nice and quiet is such a good thing.

MAMA. I understand.

DAD. But, just like you, I'm trying to keep an open mind. So ... what are you thinking?

MAMA. I'm thinking he has another ten years in school. *Some* school. He has to show up someplace between eight and three o'clock. For the next ten years.

DAD. School's a bore. Especially for a kid like Jesse who can't stand to sit there putting commas in sentences that don't mean anything to him or anybody else. "Who was the twenty-sixth president?" If he was an asshole, will Jesse even be allowed to say so in class? "Attention deficit"? Teach them something worth paying attention to!

MAMA. I agree. But even if we could afford private school — the private schools don't want him. I mean, they say they want "diversity," but that just means they want different colored kids who know how to sit still and be quiet. They don't want different kinds of *minds!*

DAD. Well, too bad, they got 'em. Kids' minds *are* different now. Anything they're asked to memorize, they can get on the computer faster — and that's what their minds want — faster! — so what do they need a bunch of meaningless facts stored in their heads for? So they can get a good grade on a test? Get a PhD? What for? So we can convince ourselves we're as smart as the Indians or the Chinese, who are taking our jobs anyway? "No Child Left Behind"? The whole country's been left behind! *(He starts to look for something.)* Where is the goddam — ?

MAMA. I know, honey, but *our* child is the one being "recommended" for special ed!

DAD. Special ed? Special ed is like preschool for jail! *(He continues looking …)*

MAMA. Well, either the school system has to change. Or Jesse does. *(With great difficulty.)* What's worse? Giving a child a drug? Or having him go to school day after day, year after year, hearing his name called out like a curse, seeing the smiles on teachers' faces turn to frowns. Do you think he's falling off desks to make people laugh because he's having a good time? Face it, honey, the school system is not going to smile on our child.

DAD. So you would drug our child to fit into a school system that is not only outdated but unkind?

MAMA. It's not just school. He has to be able to get along with friends! *(He finds the TV remote and starts to program.)* You can't get tired of a game after two minutes and expect your friend to just switch games with you happily. You can't just turn on the TV in the middle of a conversation with a friend —

DAD. I'm just Tivo-ing something —

MAMA. You can't just tivo in the middle of a painful discussion — or the other person will feel that you're not PAYING ATTENTION TO THEM!

DAD. I'm Tivo-ing so I *can* pay attention!

MAMA. Can't you wait?! Can't you just sit still and have a conversation? Can't you just — sit still?

DAD. *(Incredulous.)* Look who's talking! You can't meditate for five minutes! Can't get through a phone call without succumbing to call waiting five times! You can't finish one dining room to help pay for all the — *(He bumps into a big pile of shoe boxes from Zappos.)* And what are all these goddamn shoes?!

MAMA. I'm returning them! You always have to start a fight, don't you? You know *why* you always have to start a fight? Because you're trying to get your pre-frontal cortex up! That's why! And if you'd been paying attention the first time I tried to explain it to you, you'd know it was because YOU HAVE ADD!

DAD. *(Laughs.)* I have ADD?

MAMA. Which is HEREDITARY! Which is why our son has it!

DAD. Oh! It's hereditary and I gave it to him? He's gotten it from MY SIDE?

MAMA. It's not your fault.

DAD. Okay. You want to talk about ADD? Let's talk about *ADD.*

MAMA. Sure, now that your prefrontal cortex is sufficiently stimulated to have the discussion!

DAD. Let's talk about ADD. Let's talk about your mother! Can a person get a word in edgewise with the woman? Does she ever finish a thought?

MAMA. What about your sister? I did Lamaze with her, she talked all through class! I thought we were going to get kicked out — of Lamaze! She couldn't breathe when she had the kid because she never stopped talking! Two out of three of your brothers are cops, and I ask you — what is more "stimulating" — what is more "high risk" than that? If the jails are filled with ADD, what about the police force? I mean, for sure we know they're not the best listeners!

DAD. Who is a good listener?! Tell me! Name one person we know who is a good listener. Maybe, in a rare lapse in conversation, one of your friends will pause in the middle of a monologue for — *(Imitates her friend.)* "So how are *you?*" *(As himself.)* "Well, I'm going in for surgery, actually — " *(As friend.)* "Really? You know,

50

my boss had surgery last week. Kidney stones. Oh my God, now *that's* pain." Five minutes on the boss. Another five on the shit going down at the office, the pros and cons of looking for another job … the economy, why I should read *The Secret*! — I could be dying of cancer and this so called "friend" would never even get to — *(As friend.)* "Gee, what kind?"!

MAMA. Yeah, well, that's not "ADD," that's narcissism.

DAD. *You* are changing the subject! I asked you a question! Name one person who has the attention span to actually listen. I will stand here while you — no — *(Sits.)* I will *sit* here patiently while you come up with your answer! *(Mama thinks.)*

MAMA. Well … *(Looks at audience.)* They listen! Why do you think I talk to them?

DAD. They *look* like they're listening. They're thinking about their own problems!

MAMA. Okay … Dr. Zavala. *(Dad jumps up.)*

DAD. Because we pay her a hundred twenty-five an hour! For what? To listen for hours and hours and hours and then tell us to drug our child? I love that child! That's — my boy! *(Breaks into tears.)* I love — *(Mama goes and puts her arms around him.)* I don't know what to do. I just want him to be … a happy kid …

MAMA. I know. I know. So do I … *(They stand there, holding each other. To audience:)* The next week, we —

DAD. *(Pulls away; cold.)* Not "we" —

MAMA. I … try Ritalin. *(Dad exits.)*

Scene 14

JESSE. *(Precise, focused.)* Scene Fourteen.

MAMA. Scene Fourteen? You're sure it's not Scene Sixteen?

JESSE. Scene *Fourteen*.

MAMA. We try Ritalin in the form of a drug called Concerta, which is designed to last ten to twelve hours. *(The screen changes to a blackboard with a class schedule, and Mrs. Holly comes on, smiling.)*

MRS. HOLLY. Well, I definitely see some improvement. He stays in his chair more. No fiddling. No fights this week on the playground …

MAMA. Thank you, Mrs. Holly.

MRS. HOLLY. No interruptions in class ...

MAMA. *(To audience.)* Drugs are amazing, she's like a new teacher!

MRS. HOLLY. Good job! *(Mrs. Holly smiles and leaves. The screen changes to the TV at home,* SpongeBob, *which can be a still.)*

MAMA. The first week on Concerta, Jesse doesn't eat lunch, picks at dinner, and doesn't fall asleep till one A.M. At eight P.M., around the time the drug starts to wear off, I ask him to get into his pajamas. *(Dad comes on, carrying laundry and hears ...)*

JESSE. *(Bursts into tears.)* Leave me alone! Just leave me alone! Why are you always bothering me? Why can't you leave me alone! I'm trying to be good! I'm trying to be good so we can be a happy family! *(Dad looks at Mama, then heads for Jesse's room.)*

MAMA. *(To audience.)* Dr. Jinks increases the dosage. Twice. And soon, by seven-thirty P.M., Jesse's in his pajamas. By seven-thirty A.M., he's dressed. Even on Saturday. *(Calls offstage.)* Jesse? *(Beat.)* Jesse?

JESSE. Yeah?

MAMA. What are you doing, sweetie? *(Jesse sounds rather like a zombie.)*

JESSE. *(Flatly.)* Watching TV.

MAMA. Do you want to do a water color with me? *(Beat.)* Do you want to make hors d'oeuvres? *(Beat.)* Jess?

JESSE. No thanks. *(Mrs. Holly comes on, pleased.)*

MRS. HOLLY. He completed his entire spelling challenge this week.

MAMA. He got all the words right?!

MRS. HOLLY. No, but he finished the entire test! You know, the right thing isn't necessarily the easy thing. But he'll thank you. *(Mrs. Holly leaves. Dad crosses through the living room.)*

MAMA. He's still not eating. He's pretty much been sitting there all weekend ...

DAD. Nice and quiet? *(Dad exits, heading for Jesse's room. Dr. Jinks comes on.)*

DR. JINKS. *(Caring.)* I'm going to switch him to another stimulant, Adderal. See if it lessens the side effects. *(As Actor.)* It's what I take, it's fantastic. *(He tosses her pills and exits. Mama heads towards Jesse's room.)*

MAMA. Jesse? It's time for your pill, Jess.

JESSE. *(Distraught.)* I hate it, Mom! I hate it! It makes me feel like I've got bugs inside!

MAMA. Well, the doctor says you have to give it a little time.

Then you'll feel fine.

JESSE. I hate it! I hate you!

MAMA. *(Trying to remain calm.)* Time for school, Jesse!

JESSE. *(Crying.)* Please don't make me go, Mom! There's going to be a fire drill! It's too loud! It keeps yelling at me!

MAMA. The fire drill? Is yelling at you?

JESSE. It hates me! It wants to kill me! ENH-ENH-ENH-ENH-ENH-ENH —

MAMA. *(To audience.)* He begins to pant. I tell him to take a deep breath, but he can't. His breathing gets faster and faster. He flings the towels in the linen closet on the floor — and then he does something which scares the shit out of me, breaks my heart, and makes me know I am unfit to have a child. *(Beat.)* He hides. In the linen closet. Because he's terrified. Of the fire drill.

Scene 15

JESSE. *(Crying.)* Scene Fifteen. *(The Actor playing Jinks enters too early. Sad and scared:)* Would you go away? Please just go away? *(The Actor looks towards Jesse's voice, frightened.)*

ACTOR. Should I just come on? What should I do? *(Mama's phone rings.)*

MAMA. *(To Actor.)* Hold on — *(Into phone.)* Hello?

JESSE. *(Scared.)* Mom?

MAMA. Coming! *(Into phone.)* I'm so sorry about the curtains — … Well, we can lose the fringe —

JESSE. Mom?

MAMA. *(Into phone.)* Or I'll just have them made over — *(Hears she is fired.)* Of course … I understand … I'll return your last payment tomorrow. *(She puts down the phone.)*

ACTOR. So?

MAMA. Go.

DR. JINKS. When a stimulant medication doesn't work, or when there are highly unusual side effects such as we have here, it often indicates there is a co-morbid condition.

MAMA. Co-morbid? What's that? Like — a really depressing friend? *(The Actor notices that* SpongeBob *is still there.)*

ACTOR. *(Annoyed; thrown.)* What — what is that doing here? *(SpongeBob is quickly replaced by van Gogh.)*

DR. JINKS. Sixty percent of children with ADHD have other, "co-morbid," conditions as well. Like bipolar disorder, depression, oppositional defiant disorder —

MAMA. But couldn't it be that having ADHD — and having to take drugs — *makes* kids depressed or defiant? Isn't it depressing and infuriating to have a brain that feels normal to you that everyone else calls "dysfunctional"?

DR. JINKS. I have no doubt. I was going to add that, in Jesse's case, it is likely that he has generalized anxiety disorder in addition to ADHD, in which case we should try an SSRI like Prozac.

MAMA. Prozac? I read about a risk of suicide!

DR. JINKS. A very slight risk.

MAMA. And it's been thoroughly tested on children?

DR. JINKS. *(Offended.)* We're not allowed to test drugs on children. But thousands of children have used it with good results.

MAMA. You know what? I think I'm going to get a second opinion.

DR. JINKS. Of course. *(Means it.)* Please keep in touch. Let me know what you decide. *(He leaves. Natalie enters. The van Gogh disappears and a loud, violent video game fills a screen. Natalie plays on a PS2, as she gives a second opinion.)*

NATALIE. *(Agitated.)* Yeah, well, they thought I had ADD and depression so gave me Prozac … Then I like cut again, so they put me in the hospital, and I started having these mood swings? So now I'm like bipolar.

MAMA. Bipolar?

NATALIE. Like I get really excited about stuff and I can stay up for days working on my music? And then I don't want to get out of bed and go to school for like weeks. So then they put me on … Risperdal maybe? And I got like really tired and my boobs got really big? That's when I got really fat for a while, remember?

MAMA. No …

NATALIE. *(Upset.)* Yeah, you do, you're just saying that. I got fat!

MAMA. Okay, you got fat for a while. Big deal.

NATALIE. Okay, well, at least you said it. And I was falling asleep in school, so they switched me to, I don't know, I think it was Depakote? Maybe the Depakote came first, whatever. Anyway, something was doing something to my liver, so now I'm on Trileptal and some other things.

MAMA. How many other things?

NATALIE. I don't know, like six? My mom's like, "The doctor has to try things before he finds the right combination, so you just have to be patient and have faith." And I'm like, "How do *you* know? All you take is Prozac! *(Furious.)* And you're like — thin!" So now I'm going to a new school for kids who are like bipolar and ADD? You should send Jesse there, it's really easy. And see, now I know I can't take drugs anymore —

MAMA. You were taking drugs too?

NATALIE. Well — not *drug* drugs … I mean I don't take like heroin or meth or Ritalin — *(Bitterly.)* like some kids. Like I had this boyfriend? He's bipolar too. He's in a band.

MAMA. Wow …

NATALIE. But he broke up with me because I wouldn't have, you know, sex … I mean, I wouldn't have like *sex,* sex … Just … You know … And then I saw him in school, and he like dared me to cut in front of all these kids? And I thought he wanted to get back together, so I did. And he broke up with me anyway, so I took sixteen Tylenol. Now he's with this girl who thinks she's hot 'cause she's so skinny? And the only reason she isn't fat like me is she takes his fucking Ritalin! He doesn't even sell it to her, he like gives it to her for free! *(She slams the controller down. No pause.)* Do you have any clothes from like the sixties?

MAMA. I have some sixties-ish things from the nineties …

NATALIE. We're having a Sixties Day at school.

MAMA. Cool! *(Dad enters, sits, and starts flipping channels on the TV.)*

DAD. Hey, how you doing, Natalie?

NATALIE. Fine. Where's Jesse? How come I don't see him out riding his bike?

DAD.   MAMA.
He's upstairs.   He's upstairs.

(Mama leaves. Natalie watches TV with Dad, a reality show about swapping wives, like Wife Swap *or* Wife Exchange. *We see the title, and a scene plays in the background)*

DAD. *(Dryly.)* I love reality, don't you?

NATALIE. Sure.

DAD. Wouldn't it be cool to have a complete stranger for a mom for a few weeks?

NATALIE. I'll say. Do you think the swapped moms have to sleep with the strange dads?

DAD. Dunno … Hope so. *(Mama runs back in with a sixties-ish blouse.)*

MAMA. Hey, do you want boots? What size do you wear?

NATALIE. Seven.

MAMA. Really? *(She gets a shoe box from the Zappos pile and hands it and the blouse to Natalie.)* Here you go!

NATALIE. Okay. Thanks. Say hi to Jesse!

MAMA. I sure will! *(Natalie starts to leave. Mama follows.)* Natalie … *(Natalie stands there holding the shoes and blouse.)* You know, I was depressed when I was about your age … Over — oh, you know, some guy …

NATALIE. What did they give you?

MAMA. Well, nothing — this was a while ago. And my mother told me it would get better with time, and I didn't believe her one bit — because how can you believe something about time before you've actually experienced … time? But I swear to you, it got better. With time.

NATALIE. Did you cut?

MAMA. No! I mean — things still hurt, of course. The war, the environment … *(Glances at Dad.)* family things … But you get used to things hurting, and it doesn't hurt quite as much.

NATALIE. So things don't get better? You just *feel* less? *(Beat.)* Whatever. *(She starts to leave.)*

MAMA. Natalie, wait! *(She gets the big Zappos carton and starts loading it with shoe boxes.)* Take these too. They're all size seven!

NATALIE. You don't want these? Why'd you buy them?

MAMA. I don't know, sometimes I just have to buy shoes! *(She hands the carton of shoes to Natalie.)* You're a girl, you know how it is, sometimes you just have to!

NATALIE. Yeah. That's why I cut. *(Leaving.)* Bye, Mr. Cara!

DAD. See you, Natalie.

NATALIE. Call me if you need me to babysit. *(Natalie exits. After a moment, Mama turns to Dad.)*

MAMA. So how come Jesse's watching upstairs and you're watching down here?

DAD. *(Dead calm.)* I sat with him all afternoon. He's been watching the Weather Channel for three days.

MAMA. *(After a beat.)* What are you watching?

DAD. I don't know. *(Mama nods. Dad turns off the TV. After a beat, he continues.)* If you continue to give my son drugs, I will divorce you, and I will fight for custody. My son is not crazy. He's not a danger to anyone, and he wasn't a danger to himself till you gave him speed. He'll get through school … like I did. He'll be the black sheep. The freak. The weirdo. But he'll survive. *(Mama is about to burst into tears. Dad gets up and hands her the remote. Bitterly:)* Scene Sixteen. *(Dad exits, passing Vera, who's out walking with her iPod.)*

Scene 16

The neighborhood is projected. Mama follows Dad outside.

VERA. What's wrong? Did someone die? *(She takes off her ear buds.)*
MAMA. No, no —
VERA. Did Jesse get kicked out of school?
MAMA. No, Vera! He did not!
VERA. Well don't get mad at *me!* I'm only trying to help.
MAMA. I know. I'm sorry.
VERA. Okay listen, I heard about this clinic in New Mexico. A woman I know from the PTA took her daughter. She said it was the most complete program for a child with autism —
MAMA. Jesse doesn't have autism, Vera!
VERA. Well, Carolyn said the clinic says ADD is part of the "autism spectrum," so I thought —
MAMA. Oh that is such bullshit!
VERA. Okay, look, I'm just trying to give you information, I don't need to be insulted.
MAMA. I'm sorry. I'm a little overwrought.
VERA. Do you want a Xanax?
MAMA. No! *(Beat.)* I'll take a half. *(Vera takes a bottle from her purse and gives Mama a pill.)*
VERA. Here. Your first job is to help yourself so you can help your child. *(Mama breaks the pill in half. Vera notices …)* Your nails are a mess, you should use acrylics. *(Mama takes the pill. Vera takes the other half herself.)* I go to a pretty good Vietnamese lady. I've tried everyone. You have to be really careful about fungus. If they don't sterilize every single instrument —
MAMA. So what exactly do they do at this clinic?

VERA. *(Defensive.)* I have no idea! I hardly know the woman! I overheard her talking and she said her child didn't even speak before the clinic, and I got her number — *for you!* They help kids with autism and ADD!

MAMA. *(Cynical.)* Right.

VERA. Look. Call me when the Xanax kicks in if you want the number. I really don't need this today. *(She starts to leave.)*

MAMA. Vera — wait. Give me the number. *(Vera sighs, comes back, and starts to look in her large purse.)*

VERA. By the way, can you get me the number of those guys two doors down from you, because their hedges are really getting out of control. They're killing my view.

MAMA. Fine. *(Vera continues looking in her purse.)*

VERA. Is one of them a Muslim, or is he just black?

MAMA. I couldn't say.

VERA. I thought Muslims weren't supposed to be gay —

MAMA. I have never read the Koran, so I couldn't say.

VERA. *(Still looking.)* Where is that paper?! I cannot believe there isn't a special compartment for loose papers. You'd think that in this day and age, all purses would have a special ... I mean, it's a knock-off, made in China like every other goddamned thing, it's not like it would cost twelve cents to put in a lousy — a pocket — a pouch! ... Should I really have to go through this every single — !?

MAMA. Here, let me help. This is what I always do — *(She takes Vera's purse and dumps the contents on the ground. Everything's in plastic baggies.)*

VERA. *(Horrified.)* What is the matter with you! Don't touch anything! Are you crazy? *(Mama finds a piece of paper in a baggie.)*

MAMA. Is this it? Can I take it? *(Vera puts things back in her bag, distraught.)*

VERA. Take it! Take it, for chrissakes! *(Mama goes into the house. Trying hard to recover:)* Okay. Bye. *(She hurries off.)*

MAMA. *(To audience.)* I call Carolyn, from the PTA. *(Carolyn enters on her cell. Clearly, she's been through a lot.)*

CAROLYN. *(Emotional.)* My child started showing symptoms of autism after the MMR vaccine. That clinic — that clinic gave me my daughter back.

MAMA. Do they use drugs?

CAROLYN. It's a cutting-edge, totally holistic program. *(Carolyn exits.)*

MAMA. I research the clinic, have a phone consultation, and go online to make a plane reservation. *(She touches keys, and dozens of travel options scroll down on screen.)* But I get a little daunted by all the travel options ... *(She goes to the phone.)* So I call Cheaptix and give them my American Express card ... which is denied. *(Into phone.)* What!? *(Natalie comes on, very distressed. It's likely she's been cutting, but Mama is too distracted to notice.)*

NATALIE. Mrs. Cara? I'm really sorry to bother you, but could I just, like, talk to you for a few — ?

MAMA. I'm right in the middle of something, Natalie, can you just give me fifteen minutes? *(Natalie waits. Into phone:)* No, I don't have another card, I don't even believe in credit cards. Look, please don't go away —

NATALIE. *(Angry and hurt.)* Mrs. Cara?

MAMA. *(Continuing; into phone.)* I'll call Amex on my cell. *(She gets her cell.)*

NATALIE. Whatever. *(She exits.)*

MAMA. Let's just say it took a while to get India on the line, prove that I am myself and not someone who'd stolen my identity — like who'd want it? *(Listens; then.)* But I paid that bill — minus the charge from Zappos! ... Well, they were supposed to give me a full refund ... No, I don't want to open a claim against Zappos. That is exactly what's wrong with our society — well, *my* society, not India — we're so busy suing each other — we're so busy suing each other for kidneys — can't we just talk to each other anymore? ... Well, if it's an "honor to assist me," then assist me! *(To audience.)* But I get disconnected. *(Into other phone; to Cheaptix.)* I'm sorry, can you just — Hello? *(To audience.)* Cheaptix has hung up. I call Zappos. *(Into phone; to Zappos.)* Yes, I'm having an excellent day ... Yes, seven pairs, and I returned them ... Because — look, I'm not going to bullshit you, I'm not going to lie — I just didn't like 'em. *(Moved to tears.)* Well, thank you! ... No, thank *you* for being so gracious! ... Of course not, when someone shows a little human kindness, I am happy to hold. *(Prays.)* "Lord, make me an instrument of thy —" *(Sound of Natalie playing her guitar. To Zappos:)* Hello? ... What do you mean you have no record of a return!? I returned SEVEN BOXES! They were right here in my living room and now they're — *(She looks at the spot where the shoe boxes lived. Then she hears Natalie's guitar and realizes ...)* Never mind. My bad. Thank you for your time. *(She hangs up both phones. The travel options dis-*

appear. Dad comes on with a pizza. Mama rushes to him. Fighting tears:) I need your credit card number to get to a clinic in New Mexico that treats ADD without drugs, and if you do this, I'll never ask you for another thing in my life.

DAD. Whoa, back up —

MAMA. They've had great success with ADD — even autism —

DAD. Without drugs?

MAMA. No drugs! It's a totally holistic, cutting edge —

DAD. All right. Calm down. No drugs …

MAMA. I swear.

DAD. *(After a beat.)* All right. Fine. We'll go to New Mexico.

MAMA. You'll go with me!?

DAD. Of course.

MAMA. Thank you! *(To audience.)* He definitely has ADD because he's great in a crisis. *(A Georgia O'Keefe poster appears on screen, something with bones. The desert light is slightly surreal.)*

WOMAN'S VOICE. *(Soft and new age-y.)* Welcome to the Tamaya clinic. Out of respect for our patients with chemical sensitivities, we ask that you refrain from using perfumes, hair sprays, lotions, deodorants, gels, and all other scents. Thank you for your consideration. *(Two Nurses come on with large, colorful "Pilates balls" — exercise balls — on which Mama and Dad sit. Dr. Karnes comes on, carrying a medical chart. He is played by the same Actor who played Daniel and Dr. Jinks. His Eastern European accent is out of place here, though he does wear cowboy boots with his medical jacket.)*

DAD. Dr. Karnes. Can you explain the BioMeridian machine that you use to diagnose the food and environmental allergies you say my son has?

DR. KARNES. Are you a scientist?

DAD. Do I need to be?

DR. KARNES. Because the truth is, I don't fully understand how it works myself, I just know from my own clinical experience in addition to reports from Europe that it does. *(The Biomeridian machine appears on screen.)* Simply put though, the Biomeridian machine measures the energy at meridian points in the body. Imbalances in various organs are believed to —

MAMA. *(To audience.)* Forget it. TMI. Too much information. We'll just cut to the chase.

DAD. Really? You didn't want to tell them some of the other things you tried before flying out here to the clinic?

MAMA. No.

DAD. You didn't want to mention the biofeedback machine you bought? Or the brain spray called "Attention!" made by the scientist that invented Ecstasy who went to jail for tax evasion?

MAMA. *(Embarrassed.)* Not really.

DAD. And why's that?

MAMA. Because I was afraid it would hurt my credibility when I found something … promising. *(Beat.)* As it has hurt my credibility with you.

ACTOR. Am I hearing this?

DAD. But I'm here, aren't I? In the middle of the goddam desert, hundred and seven degrees, our son's Easter vacation … I am right here.

ACTOR. Am I here? Who *am* I?

DAD. Please continue, *Dr. Karnes.*

DR. KARNES. You can do our program. Or try again with medication. You should know, though, that drugs, including Ritalin, can cause reduced blood flow, brain cell death, and psychosis. *(Dad throws Mama a look.)* You should know that a four year-old, on three psychiatric medications, diagnosed bipolar and ADD at two, died because her parents overmedicated her.

DAD.   MAMA.

Good God.   Oh no —

(The Actor drops Dr. Karnes' chart.)

ACTOR. Oh come on. Really? You're buying this? *(Takes off doctor's jacket.)* Well, I'm not playing this quack. *(Starts to leave.)* I am not putting down a drug that has saved my life. *(Comes back.)* What you guys "should know" is — before Ritalin? I couldn't even get arrested! Okay, I could get arrested, but I couldn't get a goddamn *job!* *(Goes to an audience member.)* Let me tell you something. I got two little girls to support, both of 'em conceived when I was drunk, two failed marriages 'cause I wasn't a good "listener" and I'm a recovered cocaine addict. *(To audience.)* Okay, maybe I'll never have a relationship outside of Facebook. But I have the serenity to accept the things I cannot change and the medication to change the things I can. *(Exiting; to Mama and Dad.)* And I'm sorry about the restaurant scene, I was trying something with the hug, so sue me. *(Calls offstage.)* Nurse! *(He exits. A Nurse enters, played by the Actress who plays Mrs. Holly. She might be from a small town in the South.)*

NURSE. Here are the foods you must avoid. Wheat, dairy, soy, corn, sugar, nuts, strawberries, citrus, and all processed foods.

MAMA. *(To audience.)* They test Jesse at the clinic for five days. *(The nurse hands them thirty small bottles.)*

NURSE. These drops address his allergies to chemicals, grasses, and molds, and are taken hourly. *(She hands them several sheets of papers.)* Here is a list of toiletries and household cleaners. According to the BioMeridian machine, the highlighted ones are fine for your son. So, for instance, Bon Ami is fine, Ajax is not. Aubrey's sun-tan lotion is good — by good, I mean good for *him* — that doesn't mean it's good for you. Jason's shampoo is fine, Aubrey's is not ... And all products *not* on his list that are in your home now must be given away or thrown out. You'll also have to get rid of Jesse's mattress and carpet, because, according to the BioMeridian machine, he's allergic to both samples you brought in. Any questions?

DAD. Uh ... *(Both he and Mama are pretty floored.)*

MAMA. Gee ... Guess not ...

NURSE. *(Smiles.)* Well, I'm sure he'll do just fine. He's a wonderful child! *(She starts to leave.)*

DAD. What did you say?

NURSE. I said, he's a wonderful child.

MAMA. How do you ... How do you know that?

NURSE. Oh my gosh, he has a terrific imagination. *(Laughs.)* He thinks New Mexico's another planet and we're all aliens. He kept holding the handle on the BioMeridian machine and pretending he was taking off on his own space ship, going, "I'm outta here! *Hasta la* pizza!" I asked him how he liked school, he said "Do you want that answer rated G, PG, or R?" And those tattoos are a hoot! Sure he's got a lot of energy, but I wouldn't want a kid who just sat around ... He's just a great kid. But you already know that. *(Mama and Dad look at each other, moved.)*

DAD. Thank you. Thank you very much.

MAMA. Yes ... Thank you. *(The Nurse leaves. Mama turns to Dad.)* You could still go out and have a grilled cheese on your own time ...

DAD. Fuck grilled cheese. If my kid's not eating grilled cheese, neither am I. *(They rise.)*

MAMA. *(To audience; hopeful.)* We fly home and throw out everything in the house. *(The Georgia O'Keefe disappears, replaced by a projection of the neighborhood.)*

DAD. *(Positive.)* So, I'm going to go tear out the carpet … *(He leaves.)*

MAMA. I go to the health food store, spend three hundred dollars, and eat an entire package of rice cakes in the car. *(Mama is eating rice crackers as Sherry and Vera enter, talking excitedly.)*

VERA. Oh my God, Sherry, you must be ecstatic!

SHERRY. I am! I couldn't believe it! We just got the letter this morning and — *(They see Mama and fall silent.)*

MAMA. Hi.

SHERRY. Hi!

VERA. *(Coldly.)* Hi.

MAMA. What happened?

SHERRY. Oh — well …

VERA. Noah got into Westerly!

MAMA. Wow! That's terrific! Why didn't you tell me?

SHERRY. Oh, I don't know … I just … didn't want you to feel bad. I knew you were having a hard time with Jesse …

VERA. *(To Mama.)* That reminds me. I just saw that woman Carolyn. You're not going to stop vaccinating, are you? Because I just overheard Carolyn wasn't vaccinating because of that crazy clinic —

MAMA. Well —

SHERRY. Not vaccinating?! It's one thing to be irresponsible with your own child, but to put the entire society at risk —

VERA. There are kids coming into our schools from all over the place! Africa — Asia — Mexico — El Salvador — Ethiopia — China — Korea — Fiji … Guam! — God knows what they're carrying!

MAMA. I understand how you feel —

VERA. Don't give me that psychobabble. If you don't vaccinate, I don't want Jesse playing with Henry, and that's final. You will never be invited to a birthday party in this town. Don't even dream of a sleepover. You know what Jackie Kennedy said, don't you?

MAMA. What?

VERA. "If you blow it with your child, your life isn't worth anything." *(Beat.)* Okay. Bye. *(Vera leaves.)*

SHERRY. Don't mind her, she means well … So how's Jesse doing?

MAMA. Well … You know, he was having some pretty awful side effects from the medication …

SHERRY. I know. But you just have to hang in with your doctor till he finds the right combination! You'll see. Noah is doing so well now! And not just in school — he gets along with friends, practices the trombone … I'm telling you, Ritalin gave me my son back.

MAMA. Well, he's … a wonderful child. We're just … exploring something else now.

SHERRY. *(Eagerly.)* A new drug? Is it Provigil? I hear the army uses it to keep the soldiers awake and it's very promising.

MAMA. No … It's a whole program, actually. Based on, well, diet and —

SHERRY. *(Taken aback.)* Diet?

MAMA. And environmental …

SHERRY. *(Trying.)* Oh! Well, good luck with that. Let me know how it goes!

MAMA. *(To audience.)* She thinks I'm crazy. *(Sherry turns to the audience.)*

SHERRY. *(To audience.)* What I *think* is that you're doing a terrible disservice to your child. I'm just shocked you'd take that kind of chance!

MAMA. Sherry? I think — each of us just has to do what we feel is right for our child.

SHERRY. *(To herself.)* Oh shut up. *(Turns; emotional.)* Do you think I *wanted* to give my child drugs!? Do you think any mother — ? My child was in pain! He knew he was different — he just didn't have a name for it! He just thought he was stupid! A dumb ass. A stinky brain. A zero. My child was hurting and I wanted it to stop. I wanted it to end. Listen to me, every day, every day that you "explore" some "alternative" … Your child is in pain. *(Smiles; embarrassed.)* Well. I surely didn't mean to — *(Looks at watch.)* Oh my gosh, I've got to get Noah at soccer! See you!

MAMA. Bye — *(Realizes; to audience.)* She didn't mention Natalie … *(Sherry freezes. She turns to the audience, revealing for a moment the enormous anguish she hides about Natalie.)*

SHERRY. *(To the audience.)* Natalie … cut again and is in a residential treatment school in Utah where she will be safe. Natalie will be fine. *(Sherry leaves.)*

MAMA. After three months on the program, Jesse still has ADD. *(Dad joins her.)* We fly back to New Mexico. Dr. Karnes — Dr. Karnes — *(They look towards the wings to see if the Actor playing Karnes will come on. He doesn't.)*

DAD. *(Improvising; to Mama.)* Dr. Karnes — says — he wants us to stay a few weeks and hook Jesse up to an IV to chelate for heavy metals. *(An image appears on screen — a room full of children sitting in leather loungers, hooked up to IVs.)*

JESSE. What the hell are those kids doing!?

DAD. He also wants to put him in a hyperbaric oxygen chamber. *(An image of a child in a hyperbaric oxygen chamber appears on screen. It looks like a space capsule.)*

JESSE. What the fuck is that!? *(Dad and Mama think for a long beat and decide ...)*

MAMA.	DAD.
No.	No.

(The oxygen chamber disappears.)

MAMA. *(To audience.)* We fly home. *(Beat.)* And say maybe two words to each other the whole way. *(They stand there, not looking at each other.)*

DAD. I'll pick up the bags.

MAMA. But I know what he's thinking.

DAD. So ... I'll go get him in his pajamas.

MAMA. He's thinking it's all my fault. *(There is a pause. They still do not look at each other.)*

DAD. *(With great difficulty.)* Actually ... I'm thinking it's all mine.

JESSE. Dad? *(Mama watches him leave, pained.)*

MAMA. But as I'm about to go after him — *(Natalie enters, startling Mama.)* I get an email from Natalie. *(Natalie wears a uniform of khaki pants and a white T-shirt. No makeup. Quiet hair. She speaks her email to Mama or she speaks it straight out. Mama might speak to her computer or into her iPhone, or the scene might be more abstract, but there is no face to face.)*

NATALIE. Dear Mrs. Cara, I came to say goodbye ... *(Bitter.)* Guess you were on the phone ... *(Mama reacts, remembering. Laughs:)* Well, I'm in Utah now! My mom drove me the whole way. She cried through like six states. Anyway. Do NOT send Jesse to this school. There's all these rules, and if you break them, they put you in solitary, just like in the movies. Anyway. Everybody has their own horse to take care of, and I kind of like horses. Way better than people. Ha ha. Just joking. Hey, guess what? I have a boyfriend! He set his parents' car on fire. He's in a band but I haven't heard his music yet, cause we're only supposed to listen to "positive" music — *(She gestures throwing up.)* I can't get calls yet, so eee me okay? Love, Natalie. *(She starts to leave.)*

MAMA. I want to call out — Natalie! I want to call out like when she was seven, riding her Little Mermaid bike in the middle of the street. But I instant-message instead. *(As they speak, we might or*

*might not see their IMs on screen. Either way, the technology still sep-
arates them. Urgently:)* I think I understand why u cut. I think it's
like saying, "I can hurt myself more than u can ever hurt me" —
NATALIE. Huh?
MAMA. Do u cut 'cause at least you're in control of the pain?
NATALIE. I have no clue. Ask mom. She's got a whole library on
me. (Lol.)
MAMA. I'm asking u!
NATALIE. Y do u ask so many ????'s. It's not even about u! U're
just like the shrinks!
MAMA. I want to understand!
NATALIE. Y? U think if you understand something, u can make
it go away? *(With sudden fury.)* Well guess what? There's this girl
here who showed me where to cut where u can't even see it! On the
back of your neck — under your hair — way up high between your
legs ... So just quit asking questions! Cause u're not gonna fix me!
U'RE NOT GONNA FIX ME, OKAY?
MAMA. *(Beat; stunned.)* I — I'm sorry ...
NATALIE. *(In tears.)* Y can't u just make me a peanut butter sandwich like u used to? *(Beat.)* I got to get off now. Counselor's here
with my meds.
MAMA. Don't go!
NATALIE. Give Jesse a hug for me. *(She exits.)*
MAMA. *(Urgently.)* Are u there? Natalie — ? *(Cries out.)* Natalie?
*(The phone rings. Reflexively, she starts to go to it. Then she stops. It
rings again. Again. Finally, she decides ...)* No. *(She shuts off the
phone. The kitchen disappears. Sound of news reports and commercials,
as in the beginning ... along with an assault of images we've seen
throughout the evening on the various screens. She looks at each screen
... and turns it off with the remote. For the first time, there is nothing
on screen. She sits down on the empty stage where she began, closes her
eyes ... and meditates.)* "Lord, make me an instrument of thy peace.
Where there is hatred, let me sow love. Where there is injury, pardon. Where there is doubt, faith. Where there is despair, hope — "
(She opens her eyes.) It occurs to me ...
JESSE. Mom?
MAMA. Yes?
JESSE. Can I come down? I can't sleep.
MAMA. *(After a beat.)* Sure ... *(Continues to audience.)* It occurs
to me ... *(With difficulty.)* What if — right now — in *this* moment

66

— the best thing I can give my son for attention deficit disorder … is my … attention?

JESSE. Are you going to pretend? Or can I come on for real? *(Mama takes a moment and decides.)*

MAMA. Yes. Yes, you can come on, Jesse. *(She goes to his room and opens the door. Jesse comes on. He looks at all the people. He looks at all the lights!)*

JESSE. Wow. Sweet! *(Moves around the stage.)* I'm not tired, Mom.

MAMA. That's okay. There's no rush. We can stay awake …

JESSE. What can we do?

MAMA. I don't know. Just … hang out? Maybe we'll just hang out together for a while.

JESSE. Sweet!

MAMA. You hungry? Want a rice cracker? *(Beat.)* Pizza?

JESSE. Maybe later. *(She goes to him.)*

MAMA. *(With sudden emotion.)* You know I love you, right?

JESSE. Even though I'm a horrible child?

MAMA. I love you, Jesse. You're a wonderful child.

JESSE. Even though I never listen and I say "fuck" all the time and embarrass you?

MAMA. Even though you say "fuck" all the time and embarrass me.

JESSE. By the time I think I shouldn't do something — I've done it already!

MAMA. I know. Me too.

JESSE. Can we put on some music?

MAMA. Uh-huh … *(Mama puts on something classical and soothing. They sit on the floor and listen for a while. But it's not his thing, and he gets antsy.)*

JESSE. Mom? Can we put on *my* CD?

MAMA. Okay … *(She changes the CD with the remote.)*

JESSE. Track six, please. *(A song like Eminem's "Mockingbird" plays, a raw, bittersweet rap for his kids with haunting traces of the original lullaby.* Jesse starts moving a bit to the music. Dad appears, and, instead of saying something about the rap, he just watches them.)*

MAMA. How's that?

JESSE. Good.

MAMA. Yeah?

JESSE. I like the beat. *(Dad smiles.)*

MAMA. How come, Jess?

---

* See Special Note on Songs and Recordings on copyright page.

JESSE. I don't know. I like a strong beat. It's just my style.

MAMA. Right. *(Jesse starts to drum. Then he gets up and starts to dance. His own kind of hip hop. Wild. Free. And, yes, there's a danger to its intensity. Mama and Dad watch Jesse dance ... Blackout.)*

End of Play

PROPERTY LIST

Candle
Cell phones
Breakfast food
Lunch food
Laptop
Grilled-cheese sandwich, paper towel
Briefcase
Wristwatch
Notebook marked "Jesse"
Office chairs
Laptop or Blackberry with notes
2 small classroom chairs
Business card
Books
Remote control
A manual of mental health disorders called *DSM-IV*
Donut
Medical chart
Tiny jar with homeopathic liquid
Handbag
Worn envelope
Bread, frying pan, kitchen trash can
Soy cheese, spelt bread sandwich
Utensil or apple to be fidgeted with
Pad or computer with notes
Paper
Salad, water
2 glasses of wine
Vitamin powder packet
Food
Wine bottle and opener
Dinner check
Cash
Design portfolio, swatches, fringe
Coffee
Bloody T-shirt
Peanut butter sandwich
Guitar

Zappos carton
7 shoe boxes
Laundry
PS2 Controller
Sixties-style blouse
Ear buds
Pill bottle, pills
Large purse and contents in Baggies
Pizza
Pilates balls
30 small bottles
Rice crackers

SOUND EFFECTS

Cell phone rings
News channels
Clomping feet
Bomb blast on news
Traffic noises
Call waiting beeps
Honking horns
Car alarm sound
Hip hop ringtone
Video game sounds
Electric guitar

NEW PLAYS

★ **AGES OF THE MOON by Sam Shepard.** Byron and Ames are old friends, reunited by mutual desperation. Over bourbon on ice, they sit, reflect and bicker until fifty years of love, friendship and rivalry are put to the test at the barrel of a gun. "A poignant and honest continuation of themes that have always been present in the work of one of this country's most important dramatists, here reconsidered in the light and shadow of time passed." –NY Times. "Finely wrought…as enjoyable and enlightening as a night spent stargazing." –Talkin' Broadway. [2M] ISBN: 978-0-8222-2462-4

★ **ALL THE WAY by Robert Schenkkan. Winner of the 2014 Tony Award for Best Play.** November, 1963. An assassin's bullet catapults Lyndon Baines Johnson into the presidency. A Shakespearean figure of towering ambition and appetite, this charismatic, conflicted Texan hurls himself into the passage of the Civil Rights Act—a tinderbox issue emblematic of a divided America—even as he campaigns for re-election in his own right, and the recognition he so desperately wants. In Pulitzer Prize and Tony Award–winning Robert Schenkkan's vivid dramatization of LBJ's first year in office, means versus ends plays out on the precipice of modern America. ALL THE WAY is a searing, enthralling exploration of the morality of power. It's not personal, it's just politics. "…action-packed, thoroughly gripping… jaw-dropping political drama." –Variety. "A theatrical coup…nonstop action. The suspense of a first-class thriller." –NY1. [17M, 3W] ISBN: 978-0-8222-3181-3

★ **CHOIR BOY by Tarell Alvin McCraney.** The Charles R. Drew Prep School for Boys is dedicated to the creation of strong, ethical black men. Pharus wants nothing more than to take his rightful place as leader of the school's legendary gospel choir. Can he find his way inside the hallowed halls of this institution if he sings in his own key? "[An] affecting and honest portrait…of a gay youth tentatively beginning to find the courage to let the truth about himself become known." –NY Times. "In his stirring and stylishly told drama, Tarell Alvin McCraney cannily explores race and sexuality and the graces and gravity of history." –NY Daily News. [7M] ISBN: 978-0-8222-3116-5

★ **THE ELECTRIC BABY by Stefanie Zadravec.** When Helen causes a car accident that kills a young man, a group of fractured souls cross paths and connect around a mysterious dying baby who glows like the moon. Folk tales and folklore weave throughout this magical story of sad endings, strange beginnings and the unlikely people that get you from one place to the next. "The imperceptible magic that pervades human existence and the power of myth to assuage sorrow are invoked by the playwright as she entwines the lives of strangers in THE ELECTRIC BABY, a touching drama." –NY Times. "As dazzling as the dialogue is dreamful." –Pittsburgh City Paper. [3M, 3W] ISBN: 978-0-8222-3011-3

DRAMATISTS PLAY SERVICE, INC.
440 Park Avenue South, New York, NY 10016 212-683-8960 Fax 212-213-1539
postmaster@dramatists.com www.dramatists.com